Trees of the US

TREES OF THE
CALIFORNIA
SIERRA NEVADA

George A. Petrides

illustrations by Olivia Petrides

STACKPOLE
BOOKS

0 11557 03166 9

Copyright © 1996, 2000, 2005 by George A. Petrides and Olivia Petrides

Published by
STACKPOLE BOOKS
5067 Ritter Road
Mechanicsburg, PA 17055
www.stackpolebooks.com

Printed in the United States of America

10 9 8 7 6 5 4 3 2 1

Second edition

Originally published in 1996 and 2000 by Explorer Press

Cover design by Wendy A. Reynolds
Illustrations on pages 7–10 reprinted from *A Field Guide to Western Trees*,
Houghton Mifflin Co., 1992

Library of Congress Cataloging-in-Publication Data

Petrides, George A.
    Trees of the California Sierra Nevada / George A. Petrides ; illustrations
by Olivia Petrides —2nd ed.
        p. cm. – (Trees of the U.S.)
    Originally published: Williamstown, Mich. : Explorer Press, c1996.
    Includes biographical references and index.
    ISBN 0-8117-3166-9 (pbk.)
    1.Trees—Sierra Nevada (Calif. and Nev.)—Identification. 2. Trees—
Sierra Nevada (Calif. and Nev.)—Pictorial works. I. Title. II. Series.

QK149.P46 2005
582.16'09794'4—dc22   2004058958

CONTENTS

FROM THE AUTHOR

My introduction to the Sierra Nevada came in 1939 when I was a participant in the Yosemite Field School of Natural History. The following summer I was back in Yosemite, under a ranger-naturalist appointment that offered further opportunities for field study. The many backpacking trips into the forests and high country of Yosemite National Park provided thrills of scenic beauty that, after many years, are not forgotten.

A permanent appointment as naturalist with the National Park Service was cut short by World War II duties in naval aviation survival training. During doctoral studies that followed, I saw additional summer naturalist service at both Glacier and Mount McKinley (now Denali) National Parks. My career as ecologist, however, led to research with the U.S. Fish and Wildlife Service and to professorial appointments at Ohio State and Texas A&M. Those duties were finalized by thirty-five years at Michigan State University, during which national park research and consulting were conducted in many nations overseas.

Acknowledgments

Carl W. Sharsmith was Professor of Botany at San Jose State University for several decades and a naturalist in Yosemite National Park for 63 years. At age 91, he was the National Park Service's oldest ranger, guiding visitors on nature walks until just weeks before his death. As reported by prominent newspaper columnists, he was "loved by thousands" and "survived by everyone who took one of his walks."

Superintendent of Yosemite National Park Mike Finley is quoted as saying that "Carl Sharsmith was the quintessential ranger-educator, ambassador, and protector." His fellow ranger Bob Roney summarized the feelings of many admirers when he said that Dr. Sharsmith "was an icon at Yosemite . . . the John Muir of his time."

Carl was one of my mentors at the Yosemite Field School of Natural History in 1939, and I had sent him the manuscript for this small book just days before his death on October 14, 1994. I am sorry not to have had a last opportunity to benefit from his extensive knowledge of the Sierra.

Following his death, Dr. Sharsmith's friends and relatives were most helpful in locating the manuscript for this volume. I must express my deep appreciation to Ms. Linnea S. Davis of

Albany, California, Dr. Sharsmith's daughter; to Ms. Georgia Stigall of Sunnyvale, California, a friend of Dr. Sharsmith; to Ms. Chris Edison, Secretary, Division of Interpretation at Yosemite; and to James P. Corless, District Interpreter at Yosemite National Park, for their generous efforts.

Robert F. "Bob" Fry, consulting naturalist at Groveland, California and long-time ranger-naturalist at Yosemite, provided comments and editorial suggestions that were of great assistance. Dr. Bruce Pavlik, Professor of Botany at Mills College, Oakland, California, contributed helpful advice concerning the several oak species.

Dr. Alan Prather, Curator, graciously made available the fine collection of Sierra Nevada plants that forms a part of the Michigan State University herbarium.

My daughter, Olivia, adjunct associate professor at the School of the Art Institute of Chicago, provided the clear artwork for this book. She also painted the fine color illustrations for our *Field Guide to Western Trees*. I wish to thank her, sincerely, for her fine work.

An Important Note
There are indications in this book that fruits and other parts of certain plants reportedly have been used for food or medicinal purposes. Although this information has been gleaned from reputable sources, it is included here for general interest and has *not* been verified as being absolutely true. Do not eat or take internally any part of a plant for any purpose unless it has been confirmed by an expert that it is safe to do so.

As well, this book notes that some plants were once used to disable and catch fish—a practice that today is illegal and certainly unsportsmanlike.

Remember that it is also illegal in many parts of the Sierra to collect plants for any purpose, including simple identification. The Sierra Nevada is a national treasure. Please help to preserve our beautiful forests.

HOW TO USE THIS BOOK

This book is designed for in-the-field use. It provides guidelines that will help the observer identify any tree that grows wild in the Sierra in any season, not just when the tree is in leaf or in flower. All 99 native or naturalized trees in the region are covered. These trees are divided into 30 small groups comprised of species that look alike whether or not they are actually related. Within each group, similarities and differences are pointed out.

The following chart (also shown on the book's back cover) will help you locate illustrations and information about the tree you are trying to identify. To use the chart, decide which statement 1 is true, then which statement 2 is true, and so on, until the appropriate section is reached.

1. Leaves needlelike or scalelike   **Section I, Plates 1–8**
1. Leaves broad
    2. Leaves opposite or whorled
       3. Leaves compound   **Section II, Plates 9–12**
       3. Leaves simple   **Section III, Plates 13–14**
    2. Leaves alternate
       4. Leaves compound   **Section IV, Plate 15**
       4. Leaves simple
          5. Leaves thin, deciduous   **Section V, Plates 16–24**
          5. Leaves leathery, evergreen   **Section VI, Plates 25–30**

To use this chart, you must first be familiar with the meaning of some common descriptive terms, beginning with the difference between opposite, whorled, and alternate leaves.

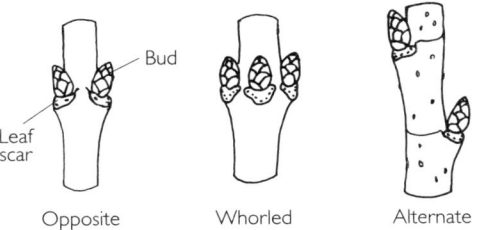

Opposite   Whorled   Alternate

Opposite leaves occur in pairs, and the leaves are positioned directly across from each other on a twig. Whorled leaves are the same as opposite leaves, except there are three or more leaves ringing the twig. Alternate leaves are staggered along

7

opposite sides of a twig; they are not directly across from each other. Remember that when leaves are absent, a specimen can still be categorized as alternate, whorled, or opposite by the positions of the leaf scars and buds.

The chart also differentiates between simple and compound leaves. A simple leaf has a single broad blade with a central midrib. The basal, or lowermost, portion of the midrib forms the leafstalk, which is attached to the twig. (The leafstalk is for the most part not woody and can be easily detached from the woody twig.) A compound leaf also has a midrib, but a number of separate leaflets are attached to it.

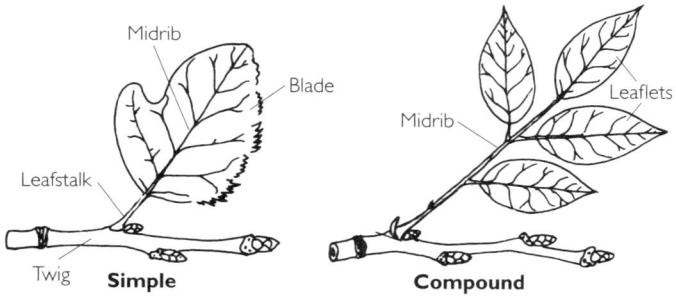

Simple   **Compound**

Compound leaves can be further identified as feather-compound, fan-compound, or twice-compound, according to the arrangement of the leaflets.

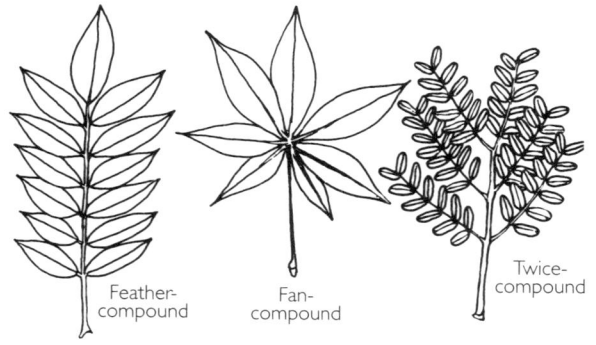

Feather-compound   Fan-compound   Twice-compound

When a leafstalk separates from the twig, it leaves a leaf scar that contains tiny dots, known as bundle scars, that can be seen easily with a hand lens; a bud also normally remains nearby.

But when a leaflet becomes detached from a midrib only an indefinite mark of attachment is evident and no bud is present.

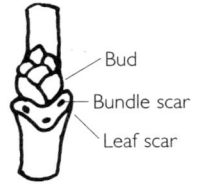

In this book, "twig" refers only to the end portion of a small branch, the part that constitutes the newest growth. A branchlet is the previous year's growth, separated from the twig by a series of encircling end-bud scars. "Branchlet" is also used here to mean any small branch that is not a twig. Short branchlets with closely positioned leaves and leaf scars are known as spur branches.

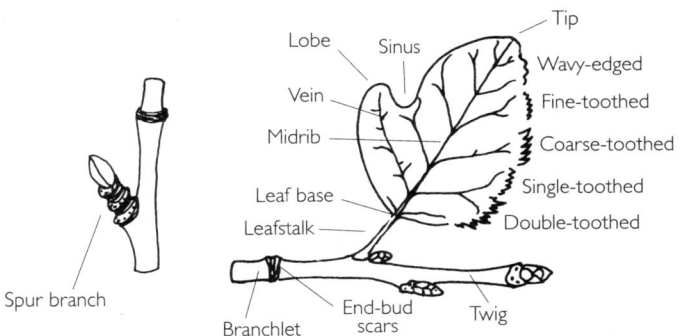

Other useful identifying features are the shape of the leaf edge; the number of bud scales and bundle scars; and the characteristics of the buds, pith, and leaf and stipule scars. The drawings on the next page illustrate these features.

This book follows the U.S. Forest Service definition of a tree: a woody plant at least 13 feet tall with a single trunk at least 3 inches in diameter at breast height. Trees not described as evergreen can be assumed to be deciduous. Within the text botanical terms are avoided; simple language is used throughout. Nevertheless, scientific as well as common names are given so that descriptions in other books can be compared.

Identifying Unknown Trees

Collecting plants for identification and study is a practice that has long been sanctioned by science. Collections should be made, however, only in moderation and under suitable conditions. Wild plant collection must be balanced against the need

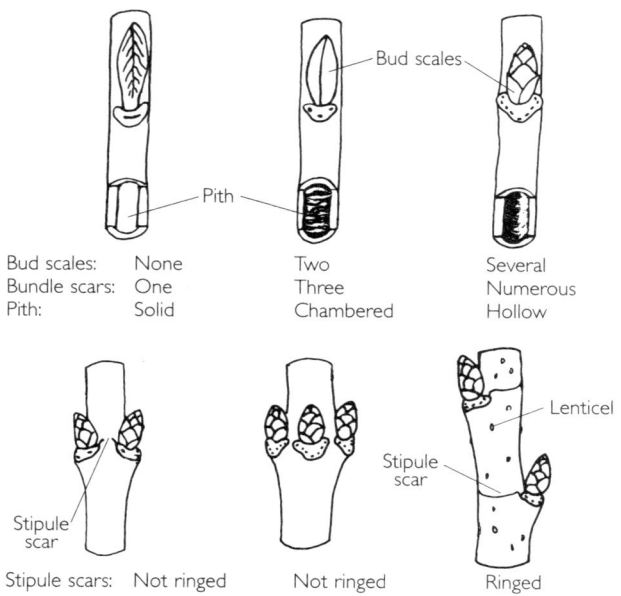

Bud scales:	None	Two	Several
Bundle scars:	One	Three	Numerous
Pith:	Solid	Chambered	Hollow

Stipule scars:	Not ringed	Not ringed	Ringed

to preserve natural values. Also, remember that in some areas, including national and state parks and monuments, it is illegal to collect plants without a permit.

Remember, too, that it is often easier to make an accurate identification in the field than it is to make one from a collected specimen. A number of important characteristics—milky sap, spicy odors, bark pattern, growth habits, and fallen leaves and fruits—are more obvious when you examine a whole living tree than they are when you look at a collected specimen.

If you do want to collect a specimen for later study and it is appropriate to do so, keep in mind that a good specimen is essential for correct identification. Avoid twisted, dwarfed, and gnarled branches. From a vigorous branch, clip from six inches to a foot of the branch tip so that both leaf and twig characteristics are present.

With the unknown tree or specimen at hand, use the chart to lead you to the proper section of this book, then scan the plates in that section to find the species that most resembles your tree. When leaves are absent, use the leafless key on pages 74–75 as well as the plate illustrations and text descriptions.

Fortunately, the field identification of trees requires a minimum of equipment: only a field guide and a hand lens are needed. A good hand lens is as essential to the botanical naturalist as binoculars are to the birder. Suitable hand lenses can be found at nature centers or any other place that sells optical equipment. A lens that magnifies 6x to 10x will not only disclose the beauty hidden in small blossoms but will be of great help in checking on the hairiness of leaves and twigs, the presence or absence of leafstalk glands, and other tiny details. Holding the lens close to your eye makes it almost part of you and usually enhances your field of vision.

Plant Names
In this book, common names that include the name of another unrelated group—Douglas-fir or Tanoak, for example—are either hyphenated or joined together to indicate that they are not true members of the group.

Although common names are well established for some species, such names often vary from one part of the country to another—and from one book to another. Because of this, scientific names are used to provide a standardized designation for a given species.

Scientific names have three essential parts: the name of the genus (plural *genera*), the name of the species (plural *species*), and the name, often abbreviated, of the botanist or botanists who assigned the name and stand as the authority behind it. Of the two Latinized terms, only the first name (the generic) is capitalized. An example is the scientific name for Pacific Dogwood: *Cornus nuttallii* Audubon.

Unfortunately, scientific names also may change as continued study indicates that a species is more closely related to members of a different group, that plants once thought to be two separate species should be combined as varieties of one species, or that a species originally thought to be new has already been named, and so forth.

Explaining the complicated rules of scientific nomenclature is beyond the scope of this book. To the amateur naturalist the principal value of scientific names is to ensure accuracy when seeking additional information about a species in other books. If both the Latin name and its authority agree, then the two books are presumably discussing the same species.

Scientific names tend to be anglicized when spoken. Don't hesitate to use them. In fact, if you call a certain plant an arbutus, a rhododendron, or a yucca you are already using scientific names. (In speech, the name of the authority is usually omitted.)

The Flora of North America, now in development, is becoming the basic reference for plant names and classification. The scientific names accepted by the specialists who compiled the first volumes of the *Flora* are used in this book.

For species not yet covered by that guide, the names listed are mostly those of Hickman (1993) and collaborators; those of a few non-native trees are from Little (1979). Unless markedly distinctive in the field (Lombardy Poplar, for example) or with names useful in cross-referencing, varieties or subspecies are not emphasized here. For full citations of references, refer to page 75.

The Jepson Manual: Higher Plants of California edited by James C. Hickman revised a number of scientific names for Sierra trees. While bringing the second edition of this field guide up to date, the opportunity was taken to change a number of scientific names as well and make various other editorial modifications. It is hoped that all of these changes have resulted in improved clarity and readability.

Measurements

Where appropriate in the text, measurements are given for tree height, leaf and bud size, and other characteristics. Trunk widths are for the diameter at breast height, commonly $4^1/2$ feet above the ground, which foresters note as "d.b.h." Measurements are given in English units. For metric conversions, see page 79.

Environmental Factors

The aggregation of trees that occurs in any locality is determined first by the parent species present and then largely by the interacting factors of climate, soil, and other living things. Temperature and precipitation affect the survival of each tree species (especially that of seedlings) and also determine the characteristics of the soil upon which trees depend for much of their nutrient intake. Other plant and animal species may cause competition, disease, parasitism, browsing, and so on.

Differences in altitude cause climates, soils, and vegetation to vary greatly between locations. Tree floras in the mountains only a fraction of a mile apart may be quite different from each other and, in consequence, support different animal populations.

Plants that grow at low elevations in northern regions of North America are often found at high altitudes further south. A person ascending a high mountain may pass through several vegetative zones, each with its own characteristic tree species, before finally reaching timberline and alpine tundra near the top.

When you find and identify a tree that is new to you it is interesting to think about the environmental factors that enable its survival, and those that are likely limiting its distribution and abundance. Shallow soil, snow depth in winter, competition from other plants, excess soil moisture, drought, lack of soil fertility, fire, insect damage—all can keep a species from becoming more plentiful. Erosion, overuse, and pollution are human factors that can have powerful effects on a species' survival. As well, glacial or other geographic events might have brought the plant to its present distribution, or prevented its spread.

Exactly which environmental factors are affecting a specific tree cannot always be identified. Insight may come, however, as you examine other specimens at different locations. It is certain that some combination of climatic, soil, biotic, and historic factors has determined the current status of the species and will continue to influence its welfare.

I. Trees w/ Needlelike or Scalelike Leaves

Plates 1-8 cover the coniferous trees of the Sierra. Cones as well as foliage can assist in identification. For pines, seeds often can be helpful, too. If not visible between the cone scales, cones can be placed in a paper bag and allowed to dry. The seeds then usually shake loose.

I. 5-NEEDLE PINES: NEEDLES 2 1/2"-4" LONG

The pines of the Plates 1 and 2 have *five* slender needles tied in bundles at the base by *short* (under $^{1}/_{16}$") sheaths. The cones are *not* prickly. Five-needle pines are also called *white* or soft pines because of the fine woodworking qualities of their lumber.

Sugar Pine and Western White Pine both occur at middle elevations (4000'-9000') mainly on western slopes. Their $2^{1}/_{2}$"-4" blue-green needles are much alike; trunk bark and cones offer the best field marks. Cones are *long-stalked*. Look for them at the tips of high branches and on the ground nearby.

SUGAR PINE *Pinus lambertiana* Dougl.
A beautiful tree, the world's largest pine and the pine with the longest cones. Cones 10"-24" long with scales 1"-1$^{1}/_{2}$" wide. Seed wing wider than the seed and rounded at the tip. Trunk bark with yellow ridges. Height to 180'-200' (220'); diameter 3'-6' (8'). Deep soils, 2500'-9000' elevations. Some trees live for 600 years. Sugary nodules form at trunk wounds.

WESTERN WHITE PINE *Pinus monticola* Dougl. ex. D. Don
This handsome tree is rather thinly scattered through the forests of the Sierra. Cones slender and *4"-10"* long with scales *$^{1}/_{2}$"-$^{3}/_{4}$"* wide. Seed wing *somewhat* wider than the seed with an angled or *pointed* tip. Trunk bark of mature trees *dark* and broken into a *checkered* pattern of small, squarish pieces. Younger trees have a smoother dark bark with a suggestion of being checkered. From 100' to 165' (185') tall and 3' to 5' (7') in diameter. Growth ring counts indicate that some trees live for 200-500 years. The clear, fine wood has many commercial uses. It is the main source of materials for the manufacture of wooden matches.

Plate 1

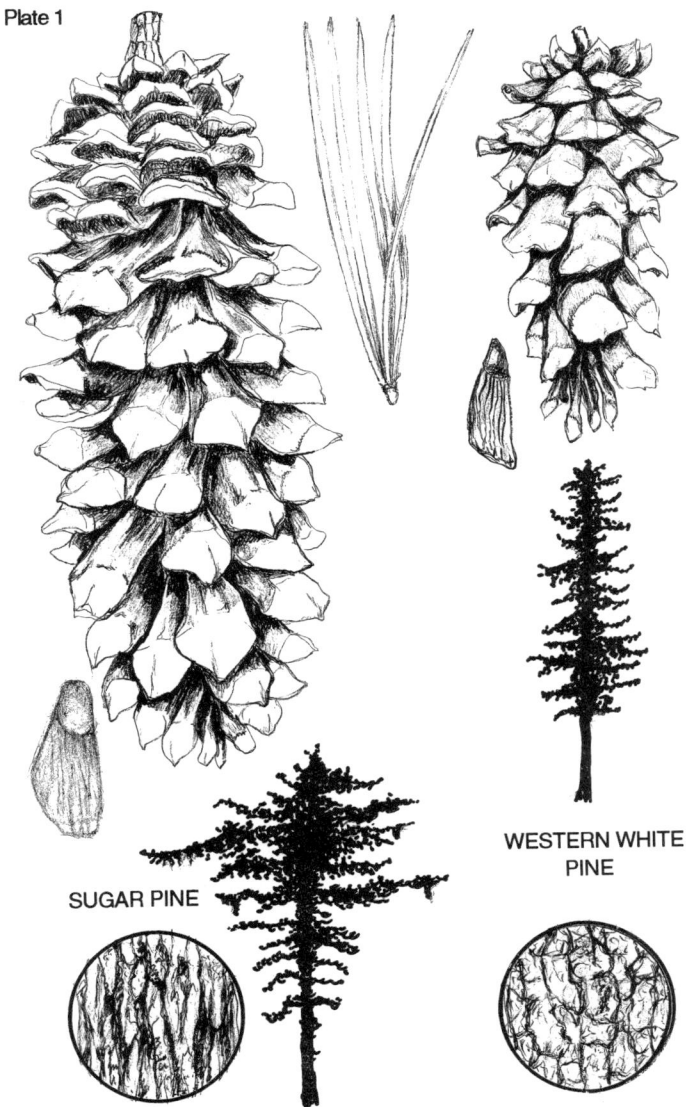

SUGAR PINE

WESTERN WHITE
PINE

2. 5-NEEDLE PINES: NEEDLES 1"- 2 1/2" LONG

In contrast to the 5-needle pines of Plate 1, these white pines have *shorter* needles and cones. The cones also are mostly *without* prickles (but see Bristlecone Pine) but the stalks are short or *absent*. Found mainly at high elevations. Lumber values low.

WHITEBARK PINE *Pinus albicaulus* Engelm.
A timberline tree or shrub growing at 7000'-12,000' elevations in the Sierra and northward. Needles 1 1/2"- 2 1/2" (3") long; twigs very flexible. Cones *1"- 3"* in length, ± spherical, dark *purple,* with thick scales that remain *closed.* Most cones are destroyed by birds, chipmunks, or squirrels. Clark's Nutcracker, a large black and gray bird of the high country, is especially active in seeking the *wingless* nutlike seeds. Even if only fragments of purple cone scales are nearby, they may help to identify the plant. Trunk bark has gray to whitish plates but is not distinctive. Height 15'- 30' (60'); diameter 1'- 2' (3').

LIMBER PINE *Pinus flexilis* F. James
Needles and twigs much like those of Whitebark Pine. Cones, however, are elongate, *3"- 6"* in length, *light brown,* and with scales that open *readily.* Seeds red-brown, *dark-mottled,* about 1/2" long, with narrow papery wings or none. Though presumably named for its flexible twigs, those of Whitebark Pine also can be twisted into knots. Mostly on eastern slopes at 5000'- 12,000' elevations. More common in the Rockies.

FOXTAIL PINE *Pinus balfouriana* Grev. & Balf.
In contrast to most pines, which display needles only on their twigs and nearby 2-4 year old branchlets, those of this species and the next may be held for 10-20 years covering even older branches in long, bushy *foxtails.* Needles only 1"- 1 1/2" long; cones 3"- 4" in length, *brown,* with prickles *absent* or under 1/16" long. Seed wing ± 1" long. Occurs at 6500'- 7500' elevations only in Tulare and Inyo counties of the southern Sierra, and again in the Klamath Mountains of northern California.

INTERMOUNTAIN BRISTLECONE PINE *Pinus longaeva* Bailey
The world's oldest trees? Though not in the Sierra itself, gnarled and picturesque individuals up to 4600 years of age are easily accessible by road in the nearby White Mountains. They can be found at about 7500' elevation in the Inyo National Forest near Bishop, California. Bushy branches needles are much like Foxtail Pine. Cones 3"- 3 1/2" long, with *weak, slender,* 1/16"-1/4" bristles. Seed wing ± 3/4". (Are aspens, Plate 19, older?)

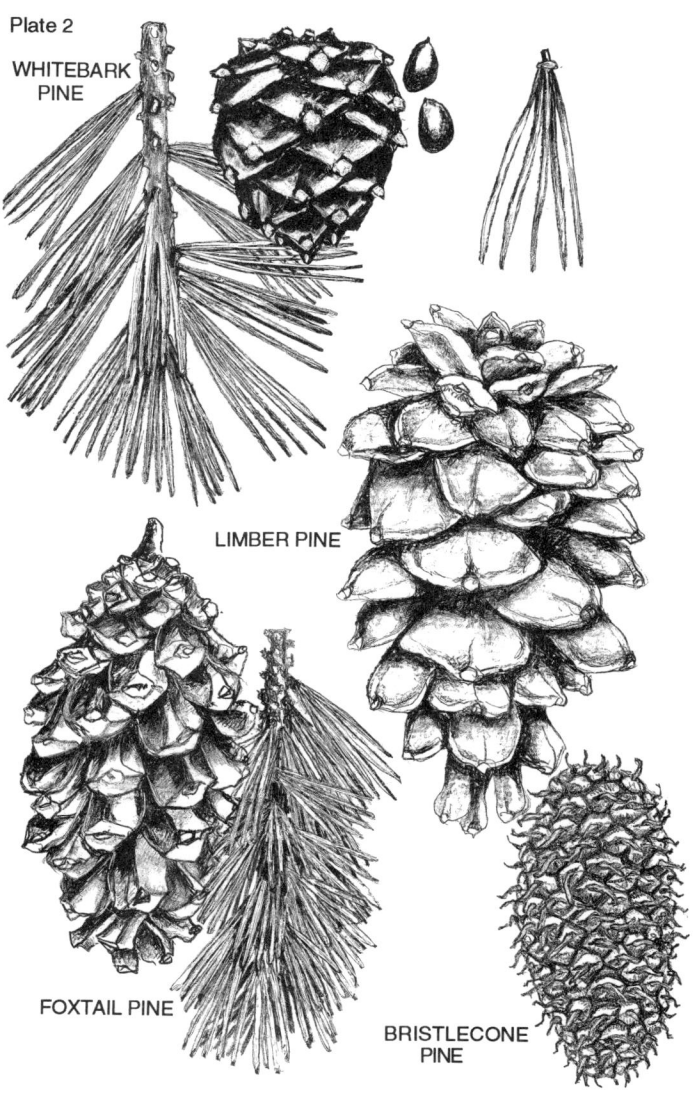

Plate 2

WHITEBARK PINE

LIMBER PINE

FOXTAIL PINE

BRISTLECONE PINE

3. THREE-NEEDLE PINES WITH CONES OPEN

These pines have *three* needles per bundle, each bundle bound by a sheath *1/4"- 1"* long. Cones are *prickly* or thorny, egg-shaped, mostly short-stalked, and with scales that *separate* to release the seeds. Pines with 2-3 needles (Plates 3-4) are termed *yellow* or hard pines. Most are important for lumber, but the wood is pitch-filled and not as suitable for fine work as that of white (soft) pines. Knobcone Pine (Plate 4), also a 3-needle pine, has *closed* cones.

PONDEROSA PINE *Pinus ponderosa* Dougl. ex Laws.
Found throughout the western states, a large pine with *5"-10"* needles and sheaths *1/2"- 1"* long. Egg-shaped cones mostly *3"- 6"* long, *dull,* with prickles mostly *curved out* and *130-140* total scales that are *dark* brown beneath. Seed wing more than twice the seed length. Mature bark in yellow plates faced with *flaky, puzzlelike* pieces. Young trunk dark, rough. Height 60'- 130' (230'); diameter 2'-4' (6'). Sunny sites at 3000'- 5000' (9000') elevations. Mule deer browse the twigs; porcupines gnaw the inner bark. Native Americans ate the seeds and used the pitch to waterproof woven containers. [Some botanists have detected a bark odor in Ponderosa trees like that of Jeffrey Pine below.]

WASHOE PINE *Pinus washoensis* H. Mason & Stockwell
Much like Ponderosa Pine; known only from ne. California and Washoe County, w. Nevada. Needles *4"- 6"* long; cones *3"- 4"* in length. Cone prickles mostly *straight;* total scales *160-190.* Seed wing only slightly longer than seed. Height 40'- 50' (60'); diameter 1'- 2' (3'). At about 8000', above the Ponderosa belt.

JEFFREY PINE *Pinus jeffreyi* Grev. & Balf.
Needles *5"- 10"* long with *1/4"-1/2"* sheaths. Cones *6"- 8"* (10") long, *shiny,* with scales *light* brown beneath and prickles mostly *turned in.* Seed like Ponderosa Pine. Mature *trunk tightly furrowed, not* flaky, but rosy or *purplish-colored* and with a pleasant *vanilla odor* (sniff in a furrow). Height 100'- 130' (180'). Mostly at 6000'-9000' elevations, especially on eastern slopes. John Jeffrey was an early Scottish botanical explorer.

GRAY (Digger) PINE *Pinus sabiniana* Dougl. ex D. Don
Needles *7"- 14"* long, distinctly *gray-green,* drooping. Cones 6"- 10" long, with *long* stalks, *uneven* bases, *downward-pointing thorns 1/2"- 3/4" long*, and weighing over a pound apiece. Bark grayish; trunk usually *forked.* Foothill elevations of 1000'- 3000'. Seeds were an important food for Digger Indians, so-called because they also excavated herb and other roots. Joseph Sabine was a London lawyer and naturalist.

Plate 3

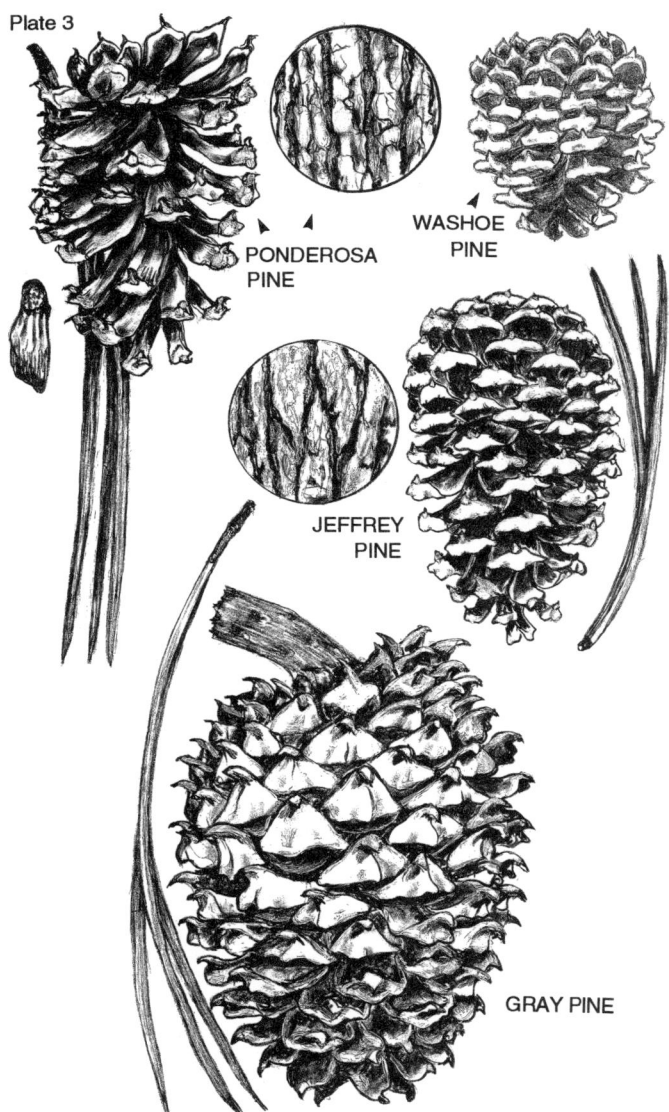

PONDEROSA PINE

WASHOE PINE

JEFFREY PINE

GRAY PINE

4. PINES w/ 1 or 2 NEEDLES OR CONES KNOBBY

Neither the tallest nor the most handsome pines of the Sierra forests, yet each of these three species has unique characteristics and values. Knobcone Pine has *three* needles and *closed* cones.

SINGLELEAF PINYON *Pinus monophylla* Torr. & Frem.
Offering tasty nuts to eat and easily recognized by its *single* needle, this is a good pine to know. The *minimal* sheath around the needle base is one of several characteristics that place the species in the white pine (Plates 1, 2) group. Needle thick, *spine-tipped,* grayish, 1"- 2 1/2" long, rarely in twos. Cones 2"- 3" long, stout, *thornless,* soon *falling.* Two nuts per cone scale, each about three-fourths of an inch long and ± *wingless.* Especially good when roasted, the nuts are much prized by people who find them before they are eaten by birds or rodents. Native Americans used the pitch to make watertight basketry. Grows to 40' in height on arid sites, mainly on eastern slopes. Other species of pinyons in various parts of the Southwest have 2, 3, or 4 needles per cluster.

LODGEPOLE PINE *Pinus contorta* Dougl. ex Loud.
The only *2-needle* pine in the Sierra (but see Singleleaf Pinyon above), reproducing in dense stands especially after a forest fire. Needles only 1"- 2" (3") long. Cones 1"- 2" in length, often persisting on the tree, scales thin and *prickly.* Mature trunks mostly with thin, scaly, *cornflakelike,* yellowish bark. Height 60'-100' (115'); diameter 1'- 2' (3'). Common at 5000'- 11,000' elevations. Seeds eaten by squirrels and grouse, twigs browsed by deer, the inner bark gnawed by porcupines. Logs and lumber used in home construction. Native Americans once used the trunks of saplings to support their teepee lodges.

KNOBCONE PINE *Pinus attenuata* Lemm.
A 3-needle, often straggling, pine with peculiar *tightly closed* cones that may become *embedded* in the outer bark of branches and trunk. Needles 3"- 6" long; sheaths stout, 1/8"- 1/2" (7/8") long. Cones *one-sided,* yellow-green, *curved,* 3"- 7" long, often first produced when tree is only 5-6 years old. Ends of some scales are enlarged into swollen and sometimes prickly *knobs.* Seeds hidden until cones opened by fire. Trunk sometimes forked. Height 20'- 30' (80'); diameter 6"- 12" (24"). Mainly northern Sierra; scattered groups on dry slopes at 2000'-5000' elevations. Lumber of little value.

Plate 4

SINGLELEAF PINYON

KNOBCONE PINE

LODGEPOLE
PINE

5. TREES w/ SINGLE NEEDLES ON THIN STALKS

These conifers all have *flat* needles attached singly by a *thin,* almost hairlike, *stalk.* Whitish markings on the needles of these and other conifers disappear from weathered or dried specimens; it is best to examine *fresh twig-end foliage.* Cones are *pendent.* True firs (Plate 6) have *stout* needle bases as well as upright purplish cones with thick, fleshy scales that soon *fall apart.* The wood of both Pacific Yew and California Torreya was valued by early Native Americans for making bows.

COMMON DOUGLAS-FIR *Pseudotsuga menziesii* (Mirb.) Franco
Needles *white-striped* beneath, blunt, 3/4"- 1 1/2" long, in *flat sprays.* Twigs *droop* markedly and show needle scars that are *smooth* and *circular,* as in true firs. Buds, however, are sharply *pointed.* Cones (usually abundant beneath the tree) are brown, woody, 2"- 3 1/4" long, with *unique 3-pointed bracts* protruding well beyond the thin scales. Topmost shoot of the tree *erect.* Trunk bark dark and grooved. Height 80'- 100' (300'); diameter 2'- 5' (14'). Named for David Douglas, an early Scottish botanist, but found by Archibald Menzies, one of Douglas' countrymen. False-hemlock meaning of *Pseudotsuga* also could be an appropriate common name. Bigcone Douglas-fir occurs in sw. California mountains.

MOUNTAIN HEMLOCK *Tsuga mertensiana* (Bong.) Carr.
A steeple-shaped tree of high elevations with the topmost leader shoot *drooping.* Needles only 1/4"- 3/4" long, growing from *weak pegs* and spreading starlike *in all directions. All* surfaces whitened; the tree blue-green. Cones 1 1/2"-2" (3") long, brown, narrow. Mainly northern slopes, canyons, and near timberline. Height 30'- 100' (150'); diameter 1'- 3' (6').

PACIFIC YEW *Taxus brevifolia* Nutt.
An often shrubby species with needles 1/2"- 1" long, green on *both* sides, pointed, and with bases *extending along* the *green* twigs. Mature fruits *bright red,* juicy, with an open end revealing a dark seed. Height 25'- 50' (75'); diameter 1'-2' (4'). Northern Sierra Nevada; forests to 7000' elevation. Bark chemicals have been found to be useful in treating some cancers.

CALIFORNIA TORREYA *Torreya californica* Torr.
Similar to Pacific Yew but needles 1"- 3" long, *stiff, spine-tipped, white-striped, aromatic* when crushed. Fruits fleshy-woody, one-seeded, *olivelike,* green, 1"- 1 1/2" long. Height 15'- 70' (100'); diameter 1'- 2' (4'). Slopes to 4000'. Also called Stinking Yew. Related species in Florida and the Orient.

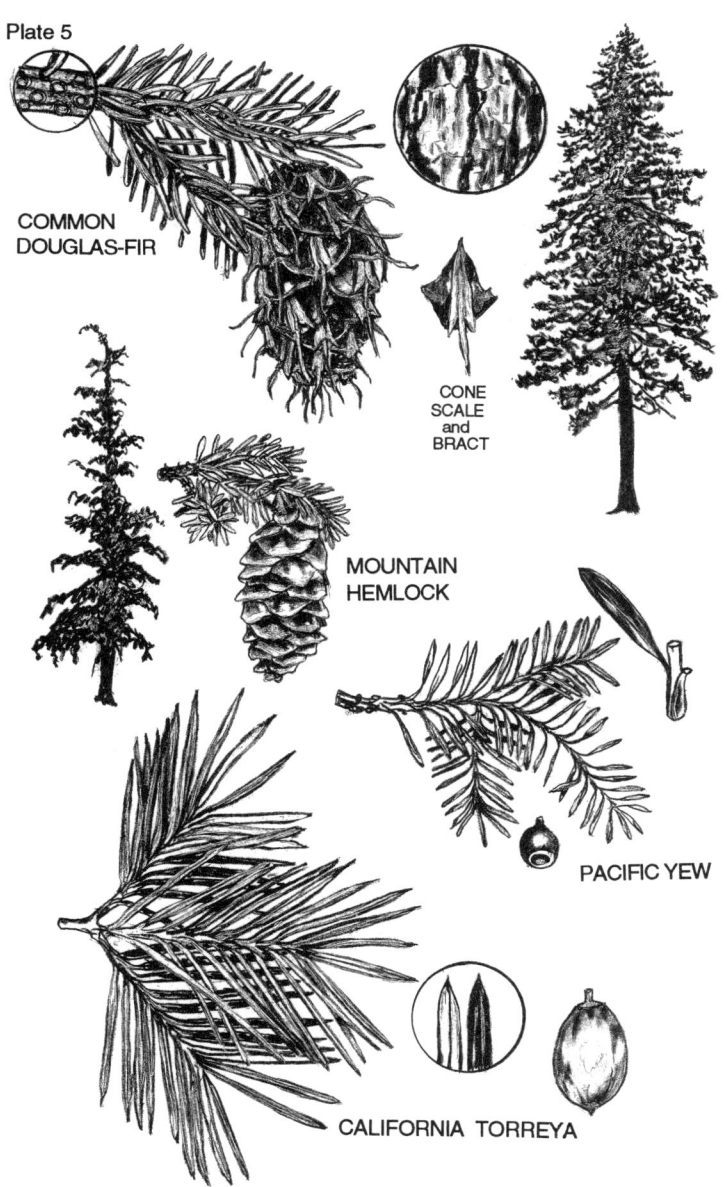

Plate 5

COMMON
DOUGLAS-FIR

CONE
SCALE
and
BRACT

MOUNTAIN
HEMLOCK

PACIFIC YEW

CALIFORNIA TORREYA

6. OTHER CONIFERS with SINGLE NEEDLES: TRUE FIRS

True firs (genus *Abies*) are steeple-shaped evergreen trees that thrive mainly in snowy climates. Needles are single *without* hairlike stalks (but see White Fir). Unlike Pacific Yew and California Torreya (Plate 5), the needles do *not* follow along the twigs but, like Common Douglas-fir (Plate 5), they do leave *smooth circular scars* when plucked. Buds *blunt* and ± resinous. Bark of young trees gray, mostly marked with resin-blisters. Older trunks darker and usually furrowed. Topmost shoot of tree *erect*.

Cones of true firs are unique but not always present. They stand *upright* and ripen quickly. The *thick fleshy* scales *drop* off, leaving an unobtrusive erect central stalk. Cone bracts are *hidden* between the scales.

WHITE FIR *Abies concolor* (Gord. & Glend.) Hildebr.
A handsome tree mainly of low and middle elevations. Needles 1 1/2"- 2 1/2" long, *flat, blunt, smooth, blue-green,* with two pale lines beneath, and *± narrow* at the base. Needles in *flat sprays* but usually curve upward to form a *shallow U.* Twigs *hairless,* cones 3"- 5" long, green to purple. Height 100'- 180' (210'); diameter 2'-5' (6'), at 3000'- 10,000' elevations.

Squirrels and chipmunks consume the seeds, leaving cone remnants in piles. Twigs are browsed by mule deer; sooty grouse eat the buds and seeds. The odorless wood was once in demand for making butter tubs and cheese boxes. The specific name *concolor* refers to the uniform color of the needles. Especially in Europe, plantings are often called Concolor Fir. John Muir called this tree Silver Fir.

RED FIR *Abies magnifica* A. Murr.
An impressive forest tree with needles 3/4"- 1 1/4" long, blunt, *ridged, ± 4-sided,* whitened *above and below*. Needles mostly *twisted upward* at the base to cover the twig tops. Twigs usually *hairy* (use lens). Cones 6"- 8" long, mostly brown-purple. Height 60'- 125' (175'); diameter 2'- 4' (8'), mainly at 5000'-9000' elevations. Called Magnificent Silver Fir by Muir.

Note: At a distance, spruces look much like firs and are commonly found with them elsewhere. There are *no* spruces, however, in the Sierra proper.

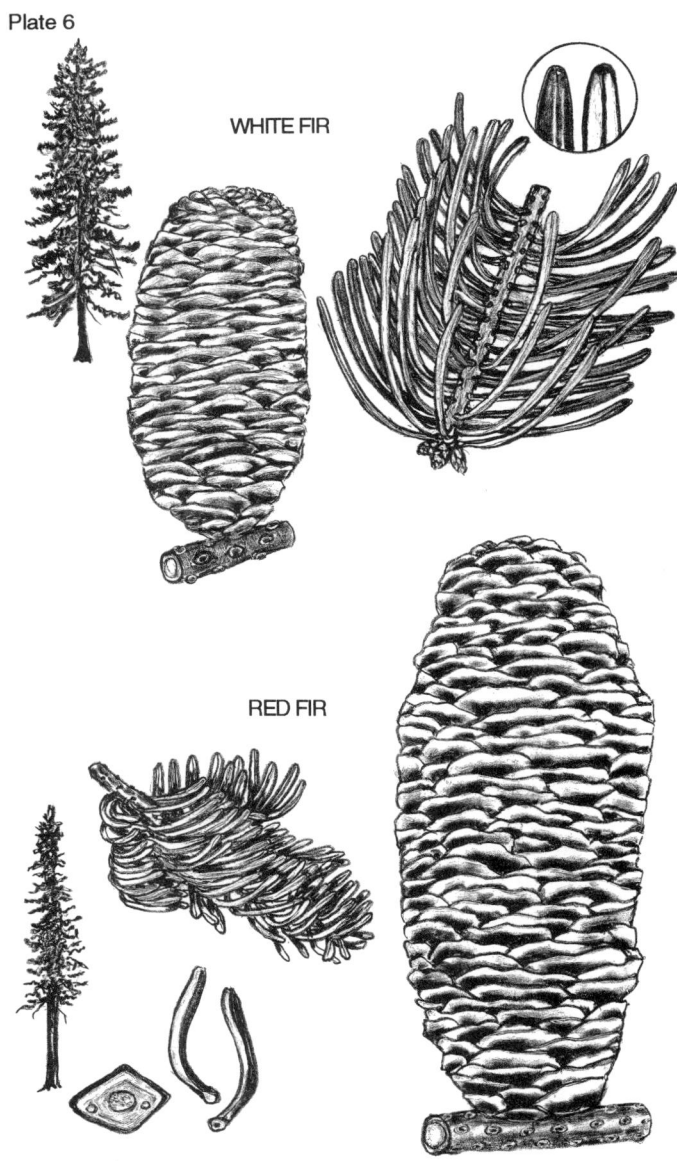

Plate 6

WHITE FIR

RED FIR

7. CONIFERS with SMALL SCALELIKE LEAVES

The twigs of these trees are densely covered with evergreen scalelike leaves only about l/4" long. Foliage is mostly in flat sprays (but see some cypresses). Cones are brown and woody.

INCENSE-CEDAR *Calocedrus decurrens* (Torr.) Florin
A beautiful large, cone-shaped tree whose smooth glossy foliage scales are arranged in unique vase-shaped whorls (use lens). There is no gland dot. Crushed foliage gives off a pleasant odor. Cones 3/4"- 1" long, slim, bell-shaped, pendent, with six brown scales, two of them quite short. Trunk bark red-brown and thick-furrowed. Height 60'- 80' (150'); diameter 3'- 4' (7'). Mainly at 2000' to 8000' elevations.

The wood is fragrant and used to make cedar chests, shingles, and pencils. Related species grow in China, Chile, and the South Pacific. The generic name is often given as *Libocedrus.*

The hyphenated common name indicates that this is not a true cedar. True cedars *(Cedrus)* are Old World trees with slender needles clustered on spur branches. Though often planted for ornament, no true cedars grow wild in the western hemisphere.

CYPRESSES *Cupressus* spp.
Unlike junipers (Plate 8), also with scalelike leaves, cypresses have *woody* ball-shaped cones. With both sexes on the *same* tree and taking *two* years to mature, cones are usually *present* on the tree being examined. A tiny *gland dot* (use lens) marks the leaf scales. Cypresses do *not* show small awl-shaped needles in addition to scaly foliage.

MacNab Cypress (*C. macnabiana* A. Murr.) is the only California cypress with foliage in *flat sprays.* Cones 1/2"- 1" wide with 6-8 scales each bearing a *hornlike* projection 1/8"- 3/16" long. Trunk gray-furrowed. Height 20'-30' (130'); diameter 1'-2'. Northern Sierra, dry slopes to 5500'. James MacNab, a Scottish botanist, collected plants in North America in the early 1800s.

Piute (Arizona) Cypress *C. arizonica* Greene, with thin *wide-angled* twigs and cones 3/4"- 1 1/4" wide, occurs on dry slopes in Kern and Tulare Counties. **Modoc Cypress** (*C. bakeri* Jeps.) is *without* either flat sprays, wide-angled twigs, or spiky cones. Cones 3/8"- 3/4" across. Rare, northern foothills.

Plate 7

INCENSE-CEDAR

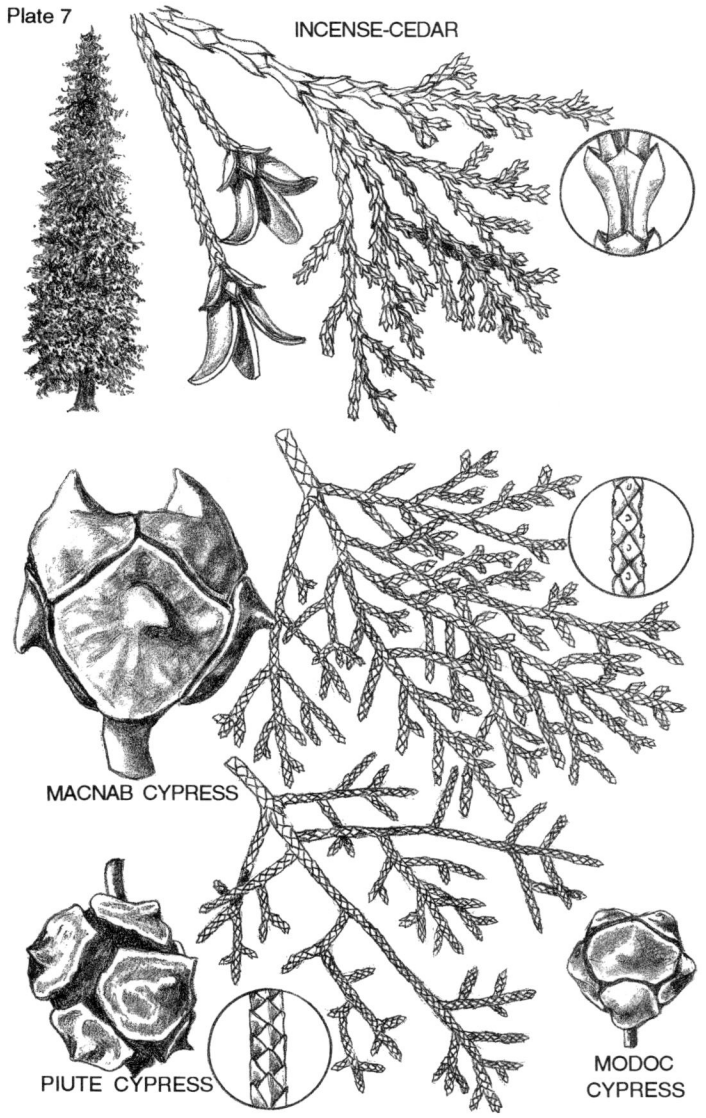

MACNAB CYPRESS

PIUTE CYPRESS

MODOC
CYPRESS

8. CONIFERS WITH AWL-SHAPED LEAVES

At least some of the small 1/4"(-1/2") needles of these species are sharp and *awl-like* (an awl is a pointed tool used to punch holes).

GIANT SEQUOIA *Sequoiadendron giganteum* (Lindl.) Buchholz

Massive and unmistakable when mature. Needles 1/8"- 1/4" (1/2") long, *all* awl-shaped, the leaf bases *following along* on the twig. Cones 1/2"- 2 1/2" long, woody, brown, egg-shaped, the *thick scales dented* at the tips. Bark red-brown, up to 24" thick. Height 100'- 250' (305'); diameter 10'- 20' (50'). Isolated groves, western slopes at 5000'- 8200' elevations.

Giant Sequoias are not as tall as coastal California Redwoods and do not attain the great age of Bristlecone Pines (Plate 2). They are, however, the most massive of trees. Before being protected in national parks, it is reported that it took 22 days to fell one moderate-size tree using the hand tools of the time. Ages of 1000-3000 years are commonly quoted. Moderately-large specimens now also grow in Europe, New Zealand, and elsewhere. Originally named Wellingtonia in honor of the Duke of Wellington, the tree is called by that name in England.

JUNIPERS *Juniperus* species

Junipers have small, blunt, scalelike foliage often gland-dotted (use lens). Small, sharp, awl-shaped needles are *also* usually present. Juniper fruits, considered to be cones with fused scales, are ± spherical, *fleshy,* and *blue or red-brown* when mature, usually with a whitish powder. Sexes mostly *separate;* male trees lack fruits. Trunk bark generally shreddy. Dried bark rubbed between the hands is good for starting fires. Native Americans and settlers ate juniper berries raw or ground into flour. Many wildlife species also consume the fruits. See cypresses, Plate 7.

Sierra (Western) Juniper (*J. occidentalis* Hook.) is the common species of the Sierra. Leaf scales *gray-green, gland-dotted;* trunk usually *single* with *red-brown* bark. Fruits of *two* sizes, *blue-*black, *1/4"- 1/2"* wide, 2-3 seeded, *juicy.* Height 10'- 25' (85'); diameter 2'- 3' (15'). At 3000'-10,500' elevations. A specimen at Sonora Pass has been estimated to be 3000 years old. **California Juniper** (*J. californica* Carr.) has *yellow-green glandular* foliage and mostly *several* trunks. "Berries" of *one* size, *3/8"-1/2"* wide, *reddish,* with (1-) 2 seeds, *dry.* Bark *brown to gray.* To 10'- 20' (40') tall and 1'- 2' in diameter. Southern foothills below 5000'. **Utah Juniper** [*J. osteosperma* (Torr.) Little] has fruits of 1 or 2 sizes, *no* leaf glands, *gray-brown* bark, and a *single* trunk. Arid soils, Mono /Plumas counties and east across the Great Basin.

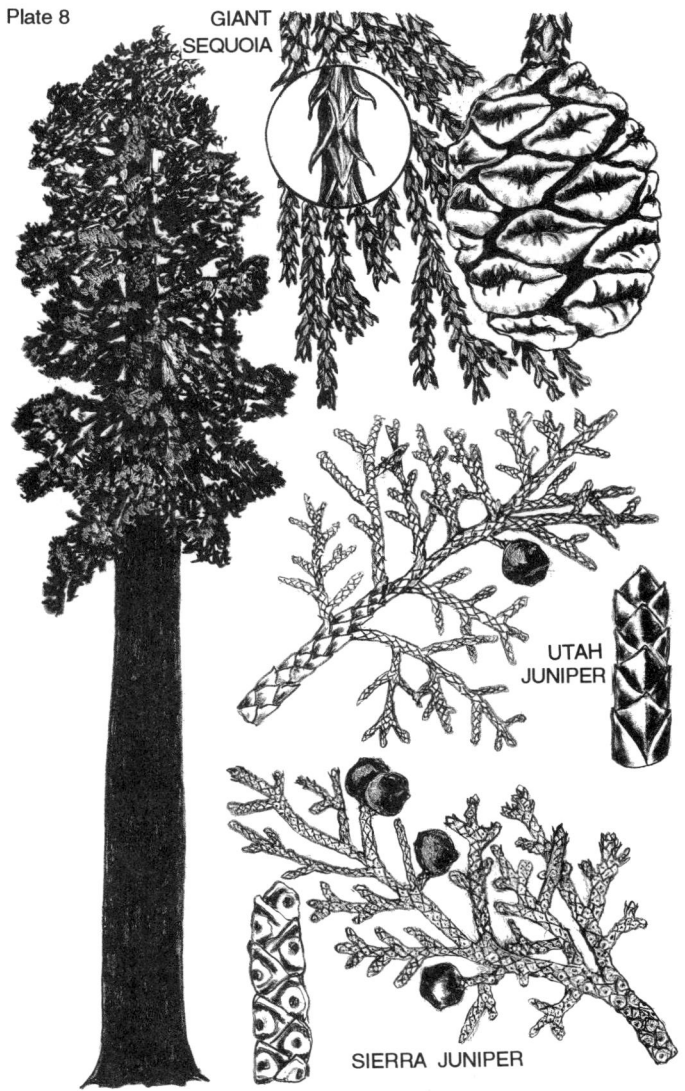

Plate 8

GIANT
SEQUOIA

UTAH
JUNIPER

SIERRA JUNIPER

II. Trees with Opposite Compound Leaves

In contrast to the needleleaf species of Plates 1-8, all other Sierra Nevada trees are of the *broadleaf* type with either compound or simple foliage. There are 14 Sierra tree species with *compound* leaves. Of these, ten (Plates 9-12) have *opposite* foliage while four (Plate 15) have *alternate* leaves.

It is essential that the leaflets of a compound leaf not be mistaken for the blades of simple leaves. If uncertain see pp. 7- 10.

Seven other trees (Plates 13-14) have opposite simple leaves. When leaves have fallen, the bare twigs of all 17 opposite-leaved species (Plates 9-14) may need to be compared (see also pp. 74-75).

9. A TREE WITH FAN-COMPOUND LEAVES: CALIFORNIA BUCKEYE

CALIFORNIA BUCKEYE *Aesculus californica* (Spach.) Nutt.
This is California's only native buckeye and its only native tree with leaflets arranged like the *spokes of a wheel*. Leaves *fan-compound,* 4"- 8" long, the *5 (-7)* leaflets each *2"- 5"* in length, toothed, and *long-stalked.* Twigs stout. Winter end bud *sticky,* scaly, and *much larger* than side buds. Leaf scars *large, shield-shaped.* Flowers tubular, each over 1" long, white to pink, in *erect clusters* 4"- 8" long, attractive, May-July. Fruits 1-2 large, brown, shiny nuts within a thick, *smooth,* green husk 2"- 3" in length. Growing to 30' in height; foothills and canyons at low elevations.

HORSE-CHESTNUT (*A. hippocastanum* L.), a widely planted European buckeye, is similar. Leaves *4"- 15"* long, with *7-9 stalkless* leaflets each 4"- 10" in length. Flowers white; fruit husks *prickly.*

The crushed fruits and bruised branches of various buckeye species have been used throughout the United States to disable fish, a practice now illegal. Buckeye fruit husks reportedly are quite poisonous and the attractive seeds can be dangerous to eat. It is reported, nevertheless, that Native Americans in some regions prepared the fruits of native species for food after passing hot water through the flour 15-20 times. (Danger: It is *not recommended* that readers attempt to do this!)

Plate 9

CALIFORNIA
BUCKEYE

HORSE-
CHESTNUT

10. LEAVES OPPOSITE, FEATHER-COMPOUND: ASHES

Unlike elderberries (Plate 11), ashes have *even-based* leaflets and small, pendent, *dry,* clustered, one-seeded, *winged* fruits. The fruit wing resembles the blade of a tiny canoe paddle. Twigs are *strong* and woody. Leaf scars are shield-shaped, contain *many* bundle scars, and usually do *not* have connecting lines between them. Buds rounded, mostly brown, with a *smooth, grainy* appearance. A central end bud is *present.* Pith is *narrow.* Flowers appear in early spring, usually ahead of the leaves. Mature trunks are dark gray with a network of fine fissures.

OREGON ASH *Fraxinus latifolia* Benth.
  Often a large tree with leaves *5"- 12"* long. The 5-7 leaflets are each 3"- 5" in length, *not* stalked, somewhat *hairy* beneath, and often *wavy-edged* or slightly toothed. Twigs mostly hairy (use lens) and *not* 4-lined. Flowers small, dark, tightly clustered, and *without* petals. Fruits *1"- 2"* long, with the wing extending over *three-fourths* of the ± *flattened* seed. Growing mainly on floodplains, some trees may reach a height of 80' and a diameter of 4'. The tree is planted in landscaping. The lumber has special values for use in making baseball bats and canoe paddles.

VELVET ASH *Fraxinus velutina* Torr.   Not illustrated
  Much like Oregon Ash but with leafstalks *1/8"- 1/4"* long and fruits *1/2"- 1 1/4"* in length, the wing *half* as long as the *plump* seed. Height to 30'. Dry eastern slopes, s. Sierra Nevada.

TWO-PETAL ASH *Fraxinus dipetala* Hook. & Arn.
  A shrub or small tree that, unlike most ashes, displays attractive *white flowers* in spring. The leaves are *3"- 6"* long, with 3-7 *hairless, sharply fine-toothed*, *stalked* leaflets. Twigs are often *4-lined* or 4-angled. Flowers have *two* petals and are *not* fragrant. Fruits 3/4"- 1 1/4" long and winged *to the base* of the seed. A tree of dry foothill slopes that sometimes grows to be 20' tall. Wood occasionally used for bows by Native Americans. When the leaves have only three leaflets, see also Plate 12. Fragrant Ash (*F. cuspidata* Torr.) of the arid Southwest is the only other American ash with white flowers; its blossoms have *four petals* and are *sweet-scented.*

Plate 10

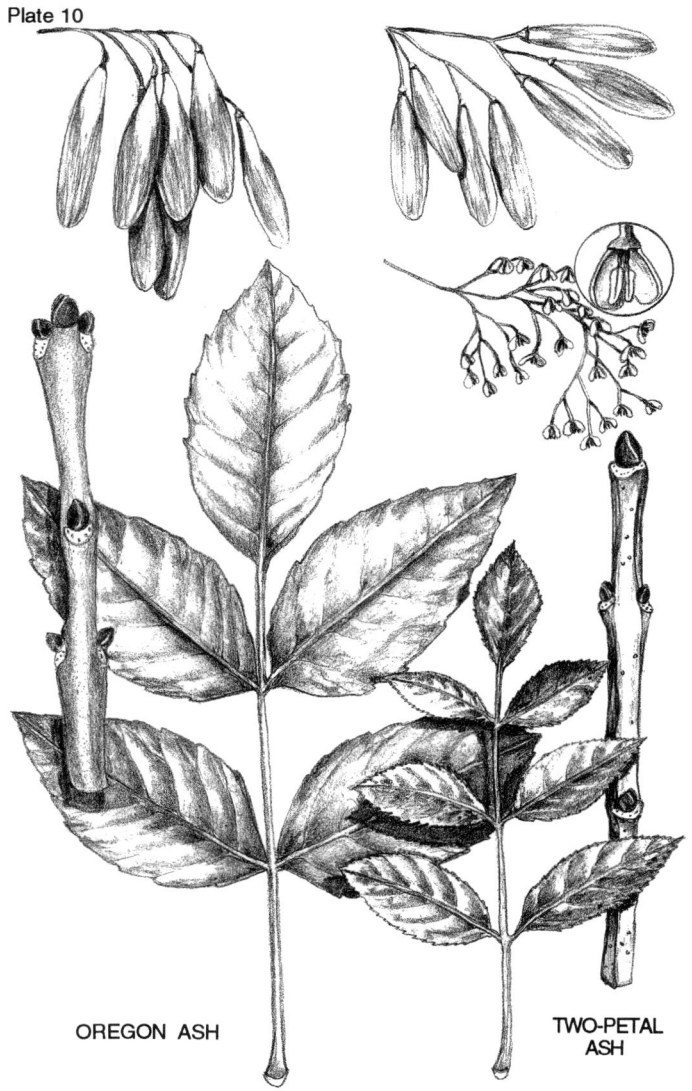

OREGON ASH

TWO-PETAL ASH

11. LEAVES OPPOSITE, FEATHER-COMPOUND: ELDERBERRIES

In contrast to ashes (Plate 10), Sierra elderberries are trees or shrubs whose leaflets have *uneven* bases and whose thick but *weak* twigs contain *wide* pith. The buds are *obviously* scaly, the central terminal bud is *lacking,* and *lines* connect the paired leaf scars. Bundle scars are 3-7. The tiny, white, summer flowers and *juicy, several-seeded* fruits occur in *±flat-topped* twig-end clusters 2"- 8" across. The blue to black fruits may have a *whitish coating.* They are often cooked into jam or jelly. When with only three leaflets per leaf, see Plate 12. The two elderberries are sometimes combined under *S. mexicana.*

BLUE ELDERBERRY *Sambucus mexicana* C. Presl.
A widespread western elderberry. Leaves 5"- 8" long with *3-9* short- to *long-pointed* leaflets. Leaflets *2"- 6"* in length, *hairless,* and mostly *coarse-toothed.* The side leaflets have stalks *1/4"- 1/2"* long. The dark but white-powdered fruits display a beautiful *sky-blue* color. Though mostly shrubby, some plants become 25' tall. Often growing in dense groups at elevations up to 10,000'. Also known as *S. caerulea .*

VELVET ELDERBERRY Sambucus melanocarpa A. Gray
Distributed mainly in the central Sierra, this elderberry has leaves with only *3-5* leaflets. Leaflets *short-pointed, velvet-hairy, fine-toothed,* and only *1"- 3"* long. Stalks of side leaflets *lacking* or under 3/16" long. Fruits *blackish .* The plant may grow to 20' in height on slopes at 3000'-8000' altitudes.

Native Americans in the Sierra favored this species in making fires. They used a dry half-inch branch as a spindle, spinning the wood between their hands. The base of the spindle, or drill, was surrounded by shredded tinder and forced into a small pit in a flat piece of dry cottonwood or juniper root. The spindle was rotated rapidly until friction caused smoke and, finally, flame to ensue.

34

Plate 11

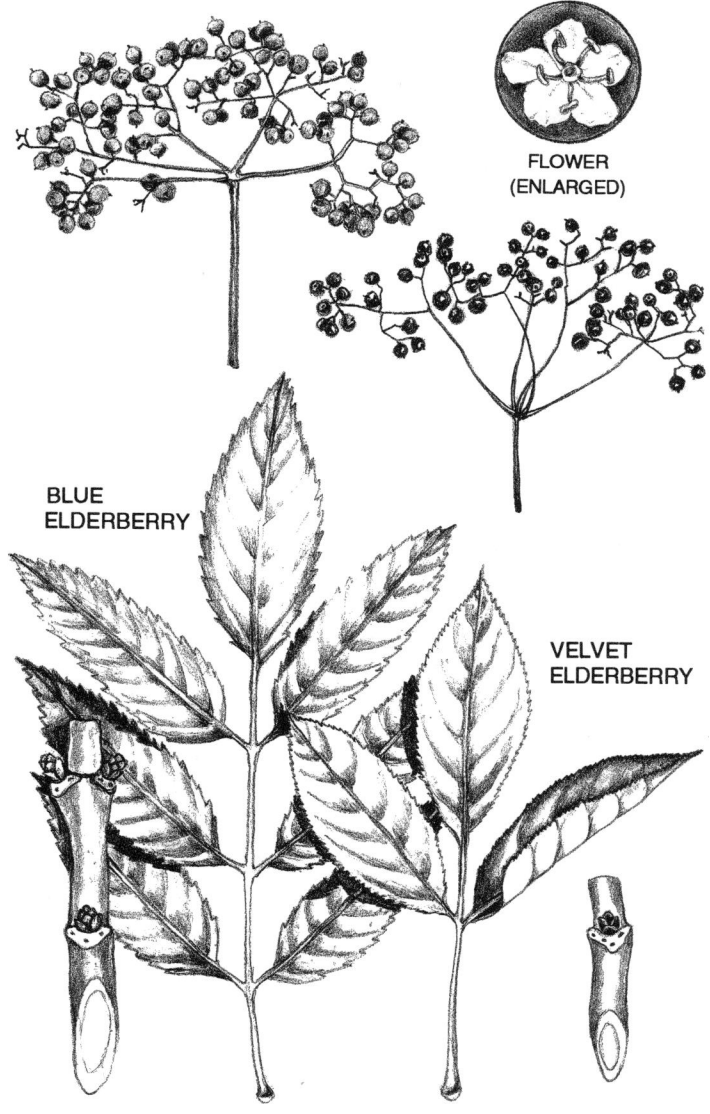

FLOWER
(ENLARGED)

BLUE
ELDERBERRY

VELVET
ELDERBERRY

12. TREES WITH ONLY THREE LEAFLETS PER COMPOUND LEAF

The three species of this plate *regularly* have trifoliate leafage. In addition, three trees of other pages (Two-petal Ash of Plate 10, Blue Elderberry of Plate 11, and Western Mountain Maple of Plate 13) *may* have some or all of their leaves three-parted. In identifying a tree with three leaflets per leaf, the accounts of those species (all with opposite leaves) should also be consulted. Unlike elderberries (Plate 11), the species of this plate all have a *narrow* pith. Note that the third species of this plate has *alternate* foliage.

ASHLEAF MAPLE (Box-elder) *Acer negundo* L.

A widespread maple with *opposite* compound leaves. Though elsewhere in North America the leaves often have 5-7 leaflets, the California variety [var.*californicum* (Torr. & A. Gray). Sarg.] is typically trifoliate. The 3 (-5) leaflets are each 2"- 5" long, often hairy, and with several *large jagged* teeth. Twigs *stout,* green or purplish; buds white-hairy; the opposite leaf scars meeting in *raised points.* A central end bud is *present.* Small, green, springtime flowers produce fruits that, like those of all maples, are *paired winged* "keys". Height 50'- 75', diameter l'- 2'; mainly bottomlands. The sap can be boiled into syrup. Foliage resembles that of Poison-oak, but that shrubby non-oak has alternate leaves. Box-elder is a poor name; the weak wood is used for boxes, but the tree is not closely related to elderberries.

SIERRA BLADDERNUT *Staphylea bolanderi* A. Gray

A shrub or tree with *opposite* leaves 2"- 5" long. The wide, *fine-toothed* leaflets, often *almost circular,* are 1"- 2" long with *tiny tips.* The end leaflet is *long-stalked.* Buds are visible, the end ones paired *without* a central bud. Twigs greenish, *slender.* Spring flower clusters white, drooping; fruits unique papery *inflated* capsules 1"- 2" long. Foothill trees up to 20' tall, at elevations under 5000'.

CALIFORNIA HOPTREE *Ptelea crenulata* E. Greene

The only trifoliate tree in the Sierra with *alternate* foliage. Leaves are 4"- 6" long with 1"- 3" leaflets *finely wavy-toothed, narrow,* blunt or short-pointed, and gland-dotted (use lens). End leaflet *short-stalked.* Buds *white-hairy, hidden* by leafstalk bases in summer and nearly surrounded by *U-shaped* leaf scars in winter. Small, green, springtime blossoms produce *flat,* circular, papery, inch-wide, hoplike fruits. Grows to be 15' tall, mostly below 2000' elevation.

Plate 12

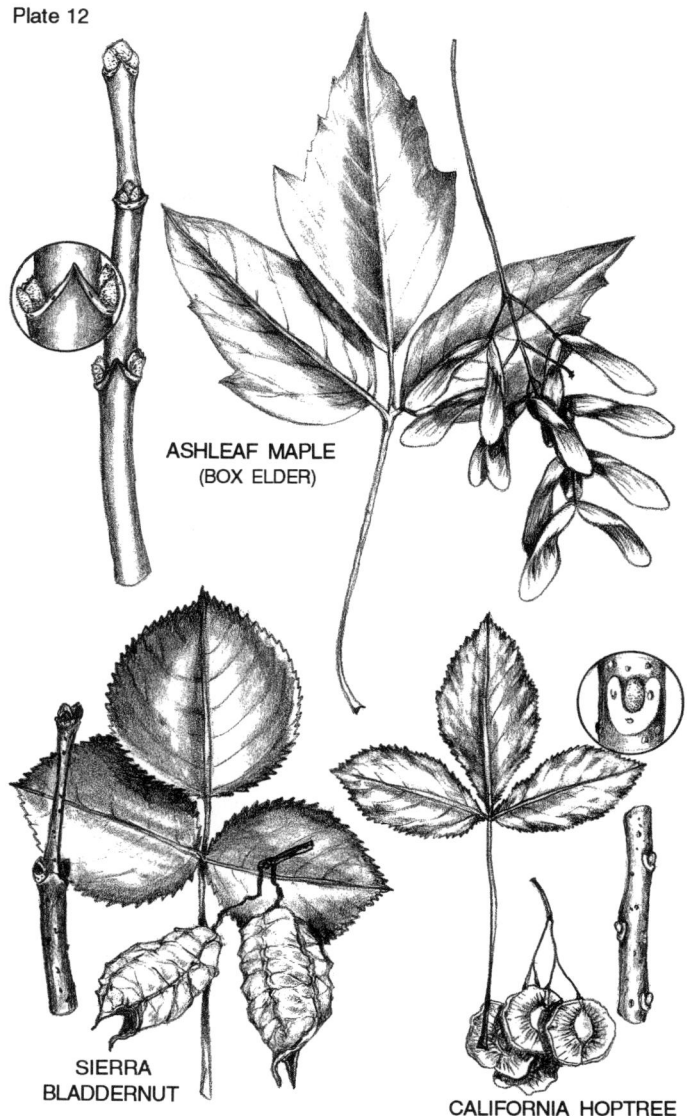

ASHLEAF MAPLE
(BOX ELDER)

SIERRA
BLADDERNUT

CALIFORNIA HOPTREE

III. Trees with Opposite Simple Leaves

In the Sierra Nevada, only the seven trees of this plate and the next have leaves of this type. California Buckthorn (Plate 28), however, may have some opposite leaves.

13. OPPOSITE LEAVES FAN-LOBED: MAPLES

In the Sierra, only maples have fan-lobed foliage and only they have the *paired, dry, winged* fruits called *keys*. The leafstalks of maples are *long* and bundle scars are *three*. California Sycamore and California Fremontia (Plate 16) also have simple fan-lobed leaves but they are alternate. The related Ashleaf Maple (Plate 12) has opposite *compound* foliage. A sweet syrup, reportedly, can be boiled from the springtime sap of any maples.

BIGLEAF MAPLE *Acer macrophyllum* Pursh
Leaves 16"- 24" long, including the 8"- 12" stalks. Leaf lobes five, each with several *rounded* teeth. Leafstalk sap *milky,* usually best seen when the leafstalk base is pulled from the twig. Twigs *stout,* buds *blunt, many-scaled.* Flower clusters *slender,* 4"- 6" long, drooping, April-May. Single fruit *1 1/2"- 2"* in length, May-July. Height to 100'; diameter to 3 1/2' (8'). Lumber used for panels and furniture. Fertile soils to 5000' elevation.

WESTERN MOUNTAIN MAPLE *Acer glabrum* Pursh
A shrub or small tree, the leaves *4"- 7"* long with 3 (-5) lobes and many *sharp* teeth. Some leaves may be divided into three rather *coarse-toothed* leaflets (see Plate 12). Twigs red-brown, *slender,* with pith *pale brown*; buds *sharp,* with only *two* scales. Flowers in *umbrella-shaped* groups, May-July. Single fruit *3/4"- 1"* long, August-September. Trees sometimes attain a height of 40' and a diameter of 15", growing in canyons and hillsides mostly above 5000' elevation. Also known as Rocky Mountain Maple or Douglas Maple. In winter, dogwoods (Plate 14) also show two bud scales. Their leaf scars are raised, however, and the pith is either white or a darker brown. Fleshy fruits also may be present.

Plate 13

BIGLEAF MAPLE

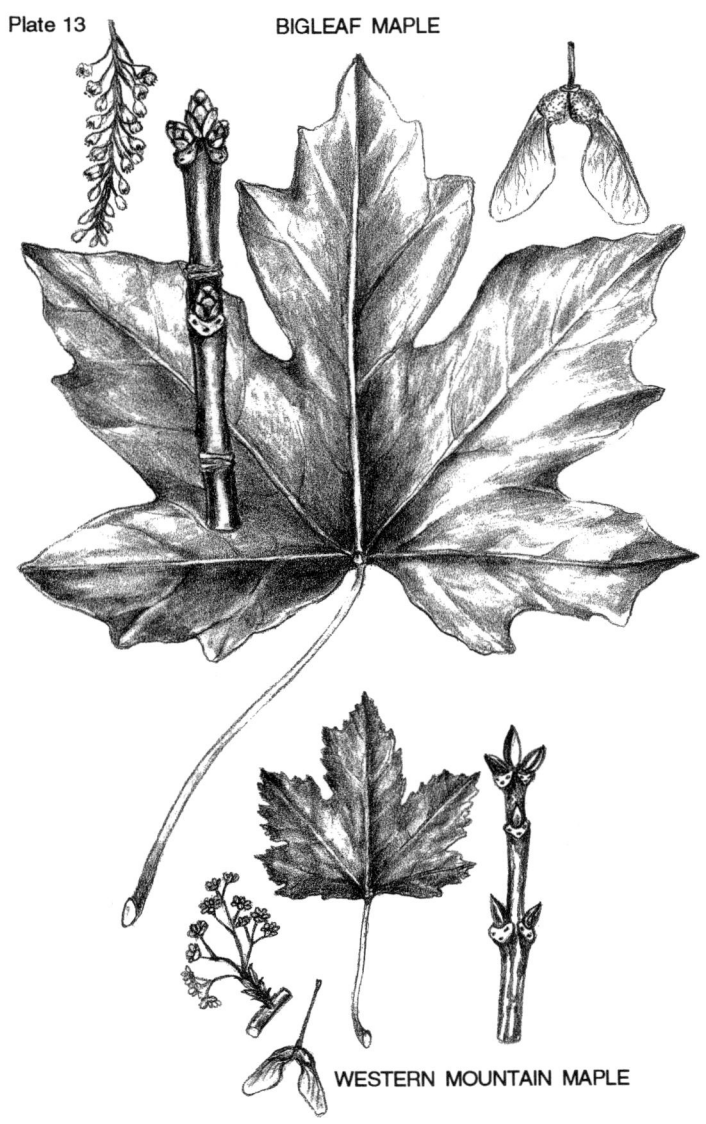

WESTERN MOUNTAIN MAPLE

14. OPPOSITE LEAVES EGG-SHAPED: DOGWOODS, BUTTONBUSH

In early spring, the white or pink flower bracts of Pacific Dogwood ffer a showy display. Most other dogwoods, however, produce only tight heads of small, greenish-white blossoms. All dogwoods have opposite oval leaves with veins that tend to *follow the leaf edges.* Leaf scars *raised,* buds *2-scaled,* and bundle scars *three.* Fruits are small and *fleshy.* Buttonbush has different characteristics.

PACIFIC DOGWOOD *Cornus nuttallii* Audubon
Leaves 3"- 5" long with *4-6* pairs of lateral veins. Unlike other dogwoods, leaf edges may be ± wavy-edged or fine-toothed. The red-brown winter twigs may show *two* kinds of buds: small leaf buds and larger *stalked* flower buds. Pith *dark brown.* Flower *bracts attractive,* 2"- 3" long, surrounding a head of tiny blossoms; fruits *red or orange.* Sometimes growing to be 100' tall but usually smaller, mainly at elevations under 6000'. Fruits eaten by many birds; deer browse the twigs. Early settlers reportedly used the boiled bark as a laxative. In winter, see also Western Mountain Maple, Plate 13.

SMOOTH DOGWOOD *Cornus glabrata* Benth.
A small tree with leaves only l 1/4"- 2 1/2" long and *3-4* pairs of side veins. Twigs droop, pith *medium brown,* flowers *lack* bracts, and fruits *white.* Height to 20', in thickets below 5000'. More frequent in coastal ranges. Also called Brown Dogwood.

RED-OSIER DOGWOOD *Cornus sericea* L.
Leaves 2"- 4" long with *4-7* pairs of side veins. Twigs *bright red* and pith *white.* Flowers small, white, *without* bracts, in flat-topped clusters. Up to 15' tall on moist soils. Northern Sierra Nevada and most of northern North America. Formerly *C. stolonifera* Michx. Shevock (in Hickman, 1993) calls it American Dogwood.

BLACKFRUIT DOGWOOD *Cornus sessilis* Durand Not illustrated
Also in the northern Sierra with *white* pith, but with only *4-5* pairs of lateral leaf veins and mature fruits *black.* The April flowers *do* show bracts but these are brownish and only about 1/2" long. Height to 15'. Wet sites below 5000'.

BUTTONBUSH *Cephalanthus occidentalis* L.
Growing in wet areas at low elevations, this shrub or small tree usually has some leaves in *whorls* of three or four. Leaf veins do *not* follow the leaf edges. Buds ± scaly and mostly *buried* in the bark. Bundle scar *single.* Pith *brown.* Flowers small, white, in tight *balls* at twig ends. Fruits *dry,* long-stemmed, in *spherical* heads 3/4"- 1" wide. Height sometimes to 20'-30'.

Plate 14

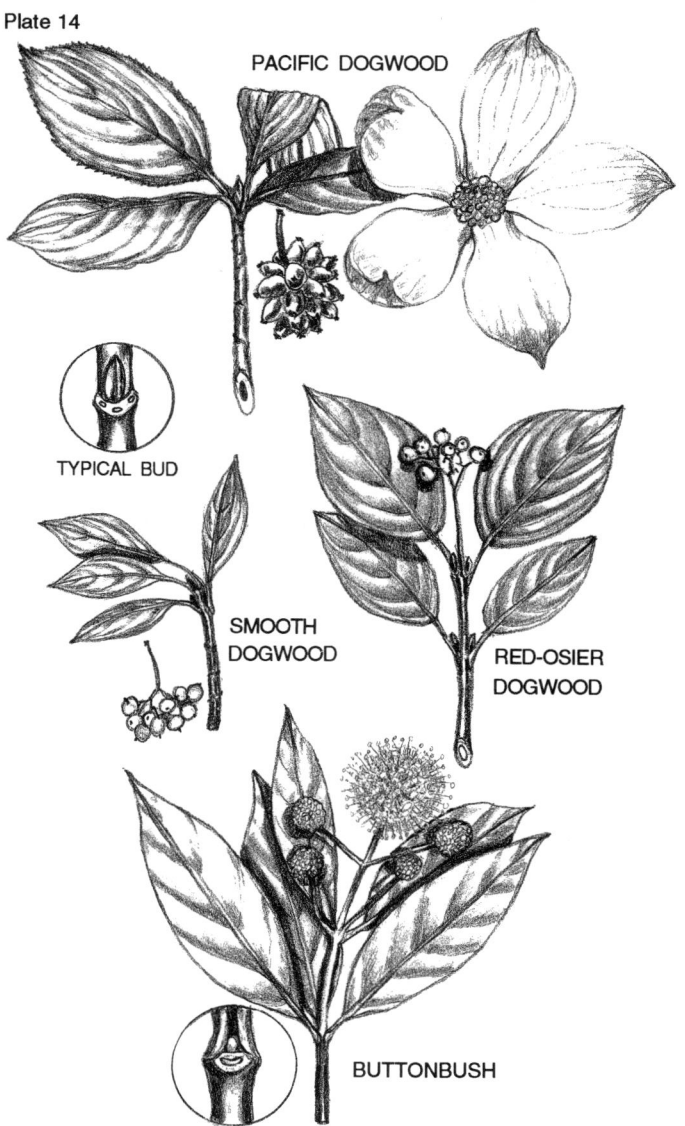

PACIFIC DOGWOOD

TYPICAL BUD

SMOOTH
DOGWOOD

RED-OSIER
DOGWOOD

BUTTONBUSH

IV. Trees with Alternate Compound Leaves

This major category involves just five species of Sierra trees. One of these, California Hoptree, has only three leaflets. It is compared on Plate 12 with the other trifoliates (all with opposite leaves).

15. MOUNTAIN-ASHES, TREE-OF-HEAVEN, etc.

Mountain-ashes are not much like true ashes (Plate 10). True ashes have opposite leaves, shield-shaped leaf scars, and dry, winged, one-seeded fruits. They have no spur branches. Mountain-ashes, in contrast, have *alternate* leaves, *crescentlike* leaf scars, bundle scars 3-5, and small, reddish, several-seeded, *applelike* fruits. Spur branches are *frequent.* The two Sierra mountain-ashes have 4"-9" leaves and small white flowers in dense ± flat-topped clusters.

In Europe and sometimes in the United States, mountain-ashes are called Rowans or Servicetrees (see Serviceberry, Plate 22). Some species grow in Labrador, Greenland, Iceland, and Scandinavia. Fruits may remain far into the winter, if not eaten by grouse, deer, other wildlife -- or, especially in eastern Europe, by people.

SITKA MOUNTAIN-ASH *Sorbus sitchensis* Roem.
Leaflets only *7-11* per leaf, blunt or short-pointed, and teeth *lacking over the basal 1/3 to 1/2* of the leaflet. Twigs and buds ± rusty-hairy. Summer flower clusters *2"- 4"* wide, June-July. Fruits *orange* or red, *3/8"- 1/2"* across, August-September or longer. Height to 20', diameter to 6". Occurs on moist soils at 2000'- 8000' elevations from central California to southwest Alaska. The species was first found at Sitka, se. Alaska.

GREENE MOUNTAIN-ASH *Sorbus scopulina* E. Greene
Much like the last species but with *11-15 narrow* leaflets whose teeth persist *nearly to the leaf base.* Twigs and buds *hairless;* flower clusters only *1"- 3"* across. Fruits *red* and *1/4"- 3/8"* in diameter. Slopes and canyons at 4000'-9000' elevation.

TREE-OF-HEAVEN *Ailanthus altissima* (Mill.) Swingle
Chinese in origin and fast-growing, but generally of little value. Leaves *12"- 24"* long with *11-41* leaflets each 2"- 6" in length. Leaflets with *only 1-2 pairs of gland-teeth* near the leaf base. Twigs thick but weak; buds small, hairy; leaf scars *large, ± triangular;* bundle scars many. Flowers small, yellow, early summer; fruits one-seeded, papery, in large clusters, autumn. To 100' tall, on disturbed sites throughout the United States.

HINDS WALNUT *Juglans hindsii* Jeps. ex R. E. Smith
With crushed foliage *aromatic* and pith *chambered,* this tree occurs at the base of the Sierra. Below 1500', near Placerville.

Plate 15

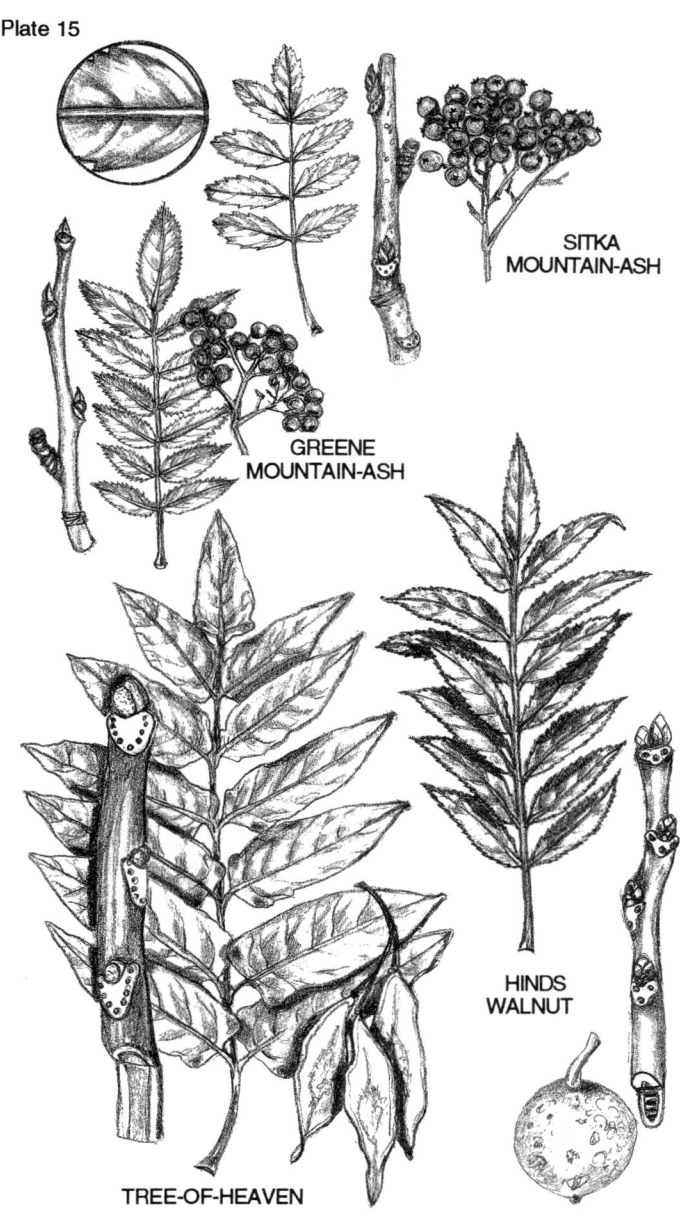

SITKA
MOUNTAIN-ASH

GREENE
MOUNTAIN-ASH

HINDS
WALNUT

TREE-OF-HEAVEN

V. Trees with Alternate Simple Leaves

Nearly half of Sierra trees have broadleaf foliage of this type. Thin *deciduous* leaves occur in 31 species (Pls.16-24) while 17 kinds have somewhat leathery, *evergreen* leaves (Pls.25-30). California Fremontia, though evergreen, is placed here with California Sycamore as the only other native Sierra tree with alternate fan-lobed leaves (but see also White Poplar, Plate 19).

16. LEAVES FAN-LOBED OR HEART-SHAPED

CALIFORNIA SYCAMORE *Platanus racemosa* Nutt.

A floodplain tree with *mottled* and *flaky* outer brown bark exposing a *pale* underbark. Leaves *coarse-toothed,* 4"- 10" long. Leafstalk with a *hollow* base that covers the bud. A leaf scar with *many* bundle scars *surrounds* each bud. Bud with a *single* caplike scale. A leafy stipule *encircles* the twig near each bud, leaving a stipule scar that *rings* the winter twig. Springtime heads of small, fuzzy, greenish flowers produce tiny, hairy, brown fruits in tight inch-wide *balls.* 3-7 balls hang on each stalk. Height to 80'; elevations below 5000'. Willows (Plates 17-18) also have a single bud scale but are otherwise quite different.

CALIFORNIA FREMONTIA *Fremontodendron californicum* (Torr.) Cov.

The only tree in the Sierra with *evergreen fan-lobed* foliage. A brightly-flowered plant with leaves leathery, mostly only *1"- 2"* long, rather *sandpapery* above, *densely hairy* beneath, and long-stalked. Usually 3-5 lobes per leaf with 1-3 main veins meeting at the leafbase. Some leaves *wavy-toothed,* others smooth-edged. Twigs and buds *brown-hairy;* buds *without* scales; bundle scar *single;* spur branches present. Blossoms *yellow,* showy, 1"- 2 1/2" across, May-June; fruit capsules hairy, egg-shaped, l"- 1 1/4" long, August-September. Often shrubby but sometimes to 25' tall; foothills to 6000'. Named after John C. Frémont, 19th century frontiersman and politician.

CALIFORNIA REDBUD *Cercis occidentalis* Torr.

Before the leaves come out, short-stemmed, red-purple, half-inch blossoms outline the branchlets and provide *showy* springtime displays. Leaves 2"- 5" long, deeply *heart-shaped* to nearly round, with several veins meeting at the leafbase. Leaf edges smooth, *not* toothed. Twigs hairless; vigorous twigs often show 1-3 lines descending from the leaf scars. Each leaf scar contains *3* bundle scars; buds have *many* scales. Mature fruits flat, brown *pods,* 2"- 3" long, July-August or longer. Flowers, not buds, reddish. Flowers said sometimes to be eaten in salads. Dried red branch wood used in basketry; roots yield a red dye .

Plate 16

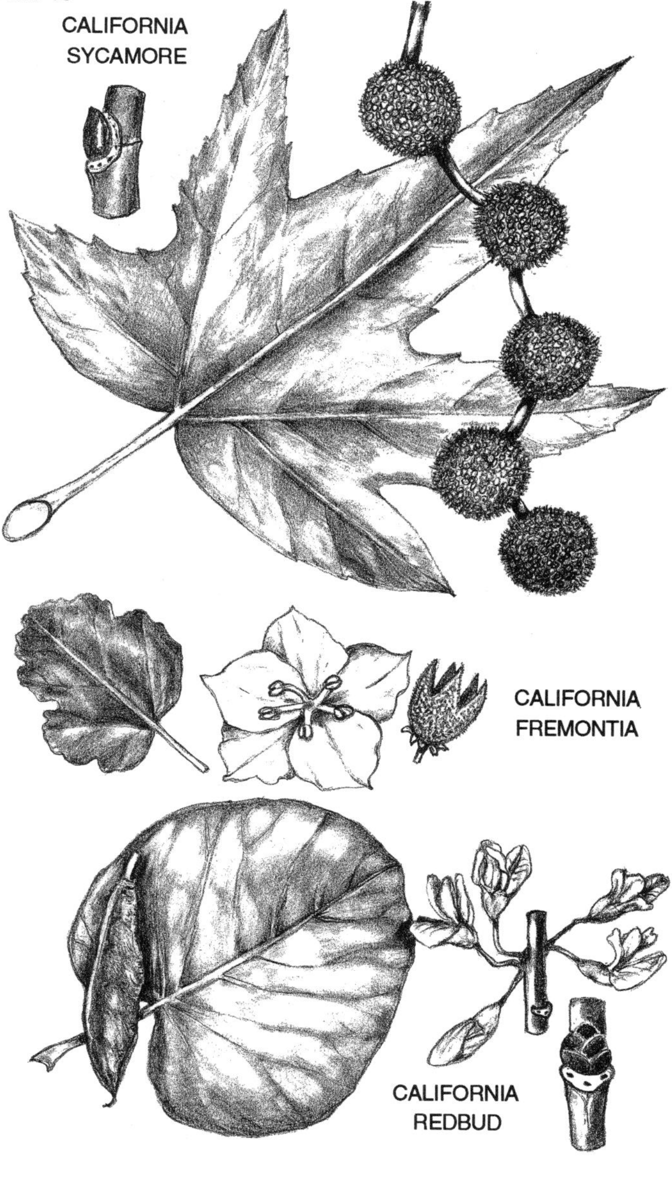

CALIFORNIA SYCAMORE

CALIFORNIA FREMONTIA

CALIFORNIA REDBUD

17. BUDS WITH ONE SCALE: WILLOWS I

Though some willows can be recognized by their slender leaves, others have wider foliage. Some non-willows (Plates 19, 29) also have narrow leaves.

The field mark that best identifies willows regardless of leaf shape is the *single, smooth* scale that covers the bud like a cap (use lens). California Sycamore (Plate 16) also has such a single bud scale, but that tree is otherwise much different. Willows have three bundle scars per leaf scar as well as flowers and fruits in slender, dry, fuzzy, caterpillarlike catkins. Most willows grow on moist soils.

The willows of this plate have leaves mostly *without* teeth and with *V-shaped* leaf bases; the species of Plate 18 are nearly always fine-toothed and sometimes U-based.

HINDS WILLOW *Salix hindsiana* Benth.
   A streamside tree with *narrow* leaves like Sandbar Willow (Plate 18) [and combined with it by Argus (in Hickman, 1993)]. The foliage is *short-pointed* and *lacks* leaf teeth. Leaves 1 1/2"- 3 1/2" long and only *1/8"- 1/4"* wide. Both leaves and twigs gray- or white-hairy (use lens); buds 1/8"- 1/4" long. Height to 25'; usually below 3000' elevation.

GEYER WILLOW *Salix geyeriana* Anderss.
   Leaves often blunt, silky-hairy, only *1"- 3"* long, *3/8"- 1/2"* wide and whitened beneath. Twigs somewhat reddish, often with a whitish powder; buds *less than 1/8"* long. Height to 15'; at 5000'-7000' elevations. Karl Geyer, a German botanist, collected plants in the West during the 1840s.

ARROYO WILLOW *Salix lasiolepis* Benth.
   Leaves of *medium width,* short-pointed or blunt, shiny, rather *leathery, ± thickened,* 2"- 5" long and *1/2"- 1"* wide. Twigs ± hairless, yellowish; buds *over 1/4"* long. Height to 30'. Mainly below 7000'. More common in the coast ranges.

SCOULER WILLOW *Salix scouleriana* Hook.
   A *broad-leaved* willow found over most of the Pacific Northwest. Leaves mostly blunt, *2"- 5"* long, *1/2"- 1 1/2"* wide, and more or less wavy-edged. Foliage *widest toward the tip,* whitish and often somewhat hairy beneath. Twigs yellowish to dark, often *drooping;* buds *over 1/4"* long. Height to 25'; growing at elevations below 7000'. John Scouler, a Scottish physician, studied plants along the Pacific Coast in the early 19th century.

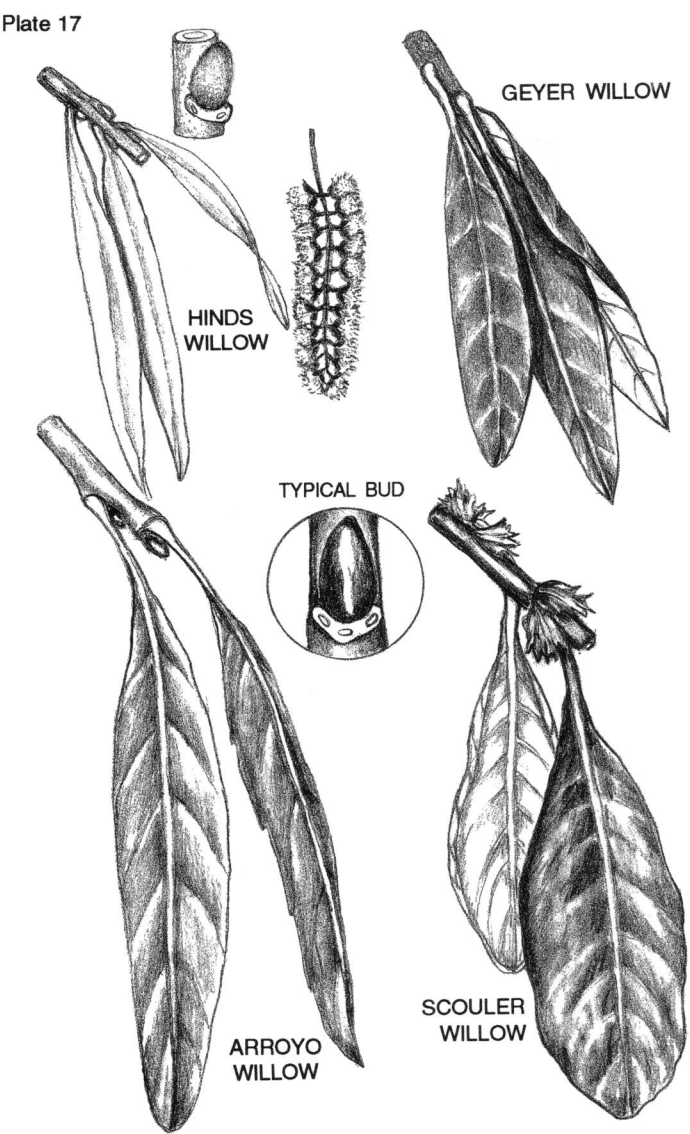

Plate 17

HINDS WILLOW

GEYER WILLOW

TYPICAL BUD

ARROYO WILLOW

SCOULER WILLOW

18. BUDS WITH ONE SCALE: WILLOWS II

These species also have leaves of narrow to medium width. Unlike the willows of Plate 17, however, they are usually *fine-toothed* with U- *or* V-shaped bases. See also Narrowleaf Cottonwood, Plate 19.

SANDBAR WILLOW *Salix exigua* Nutt.

A transcontinental species with *very narrow*, *long-pointed* leaves 1 1/2"- 4 1/4" long and only *1/8"- 3/8"* wide (see Hinds Willow, Plate 17). Leaves *V-based* and often *white-hairy* beneath. Leaf teeth often few, rarely none. Leafstalks *1/8"* long or lacking. Twigs hairy; buds *1/8"- 1/4"* long. To 20' tall at elevations up to 8000'. The long twigs and branchlets are used in basket-making.

BLACK WILLOW *Salix gooddingii* C. Ball

Another slender-leaved and V-based willow but with foliage 2"- 6" long, *1/4"- 5/8"* wide, hairless, and gray-green on both sides, stipules frequent. Leafstalks *1/8"- 1/4"* long. Twigs hairless; buds *less than 1/8"* long. Elevations to 5000'. Formerly included in *S. nigra* Marsh.

PACIFIC WILLOW *Salix lucida* ssp. *lasiandra* (Benth.) E. Murray

A willow with shiny, dark green, hairless, and *long-pointed* leaves, the stalks *1/2"- 3/4"* long. *Glands present* on the *U-shaped* leaf base or upper leafstalk (use lens). Leaves 2"- 5" long; 1/2"- 1" wide, hairless, whitish beneath, stipules common. Twigs hairless; buds *over 1/4"* in length. Height to 60'. Elevations to 8000'. Makes good charcoal. Previously *S. lasiandra.*

MACKENZIE WILLOW *Salix prolixa* Anderss.

Also with U- or *heart-shaped* leaf bases and long leafstalks but the foliage *short-pointed* and *without* glands. Leaves 2 1/2"- 4" long, 5/8"- 1 1/2" wide, hairless, and whitened beneath, stipules frequent. Leafstalks 1/4"- 3/4" in length. Twigs hairless; buds *under 1/8"* long. Height to 20'. Mainly at 5000'-9000' elevations in Red Fir forests. Also known as *S. mackenzieana* (Hook.) Barrett

RED WILLOW *Salix laevigata* Bebb

Leaves shiny, pale green, *thick*, long- or short-pointed. Foliage 3"- 7" long, 1/2"- 1 1/2" wide, and ± hairy beneath. Leafstalks *1/4"- 1/2"* in length, glands *present or not.* Twigs mostly *hairy*; buds *1/8"- 1/4"* long. Catkins *not* at leaf angles. Height to 50'. Mostly elevations below 6000' from cen. Arizona to s. Mexico, also s. Oregon to nw. Mexico.

BONPLAND WILLOW *Salix bonplandiana* Kunth. Not illustrated.

Like Red Willow but less wide-ranging. Twigs mostly *hairless;* leafstalk glands *absent; c*atkins *mainly* at the leaf angles. Se. Arizona to Guatemala.

Plate 18

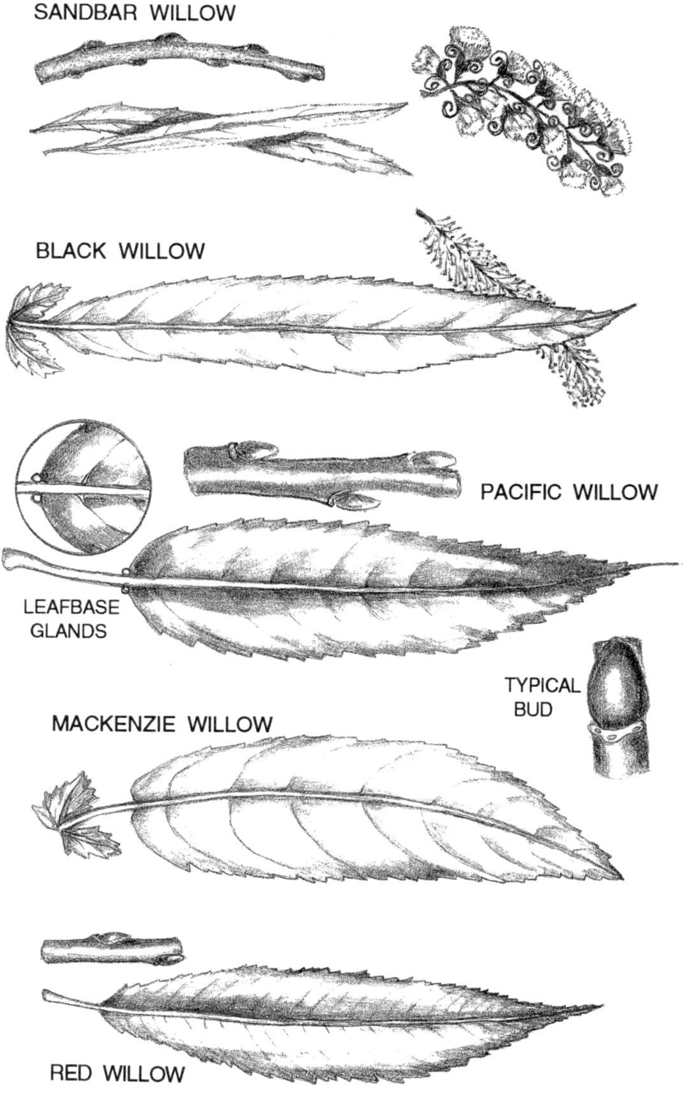

SANDBAR WILLOW

BLACK WILLOW

LEAFBASE
GLANDS

PACIFIC WILLOW

TYPICAL
BUD

MACKENZIE WILLOW

RED WILLOW

19. POPLARS: ASPEN, COTTONWOODS

The common names differ but all are closely related poplars. The leaves are broadly rounded or triangular, long-stalked, often with 3-5 main veins meeting at the base (but see Narrowleaf Cottonwood). The lowermost bud scale is *directly above* the leaf scar; flowers and fruits are in catkins. The trunks often are smooth and whitish when young. Several species have *flattened* leafstalks.

QUAKING ASPEN *Populus tremuloides* Michx.

A hardy invader of open spaces and a widespread tree over North America. Aspens spread mostly by root sprouts and estimates are made that some groves have survived for 10,000 years (far longer than other trees traditionally recognized as being long-lived -- see Plates 2, 8). Leaves 2"- 6" long with *nearly circular* and *fine-toothed* blades that become golden in autumn. Leafstalks *flattened,* enabling foliage to flutter in a breeze. Twigs *dark brown* with end bud smooth and only 1/4"- 3/8" long. Young bark *chalk-white to greenish.* Height to 75'. Mainly at 6,000'-10,000' elevations.

FREMONT COTTONWOOD *Populus fremontii* S. Wats.

This tree of the Southwest has *coarse-toothed* and mostly *triangular* leaves 2"- 5" long, generally with a tapering tip. Leafstalks *flattened.* Twigs *yellowish,* with end bud smooth and *3/8"- 1/2"* long. Mature trunk dark with deep grooves. Height to 100'. Mostly at elevations under 6,000'.

BLACK COTTONWOOD

Populus balsamifera var. *trichocarpa* (Torr. & Gray) A. Brayshaw Distributed mainly in the Pacific Northwest but ranging southward in the mountains. Leaves 4"- 8" long, triangular, *fine-toothed,* dark green above, mostly *silver-white* beneath, leafbase glands occasional. Leafstalks *not* flat. Twigs brownish; end bud 3/4"- 7/8" long, *gummy,* and *aromatic* when crushed. Height to 165', diameter to 3' (rarely 9'). Mainly floodplains below 9,000'. Earlier named *P. trichocarpa* .

NARROWLEAF COTTONWOOD *Populus angustifolia* James

Mainly a Rocky Mountains species, but local on eastern slopes of the Sierra. Leaves *willowlike,* 3"- 5" long, 1"- 2" wide, *fine-toothed;* twigs yellowish; buds *sticky.* Height to 60', damp sites.

Lombardy Poplar (*P. nigra* var. *italica* Muenchh.) is a tall, thin, *columnar* tree often planted for ornament. **White Poplar** (*P. alba* L.), also imported from Europe, has 2"- 6" leaves deeply lobed or triangular. Foliage, twigs, and buds are *white-woolly* .

Plate 19

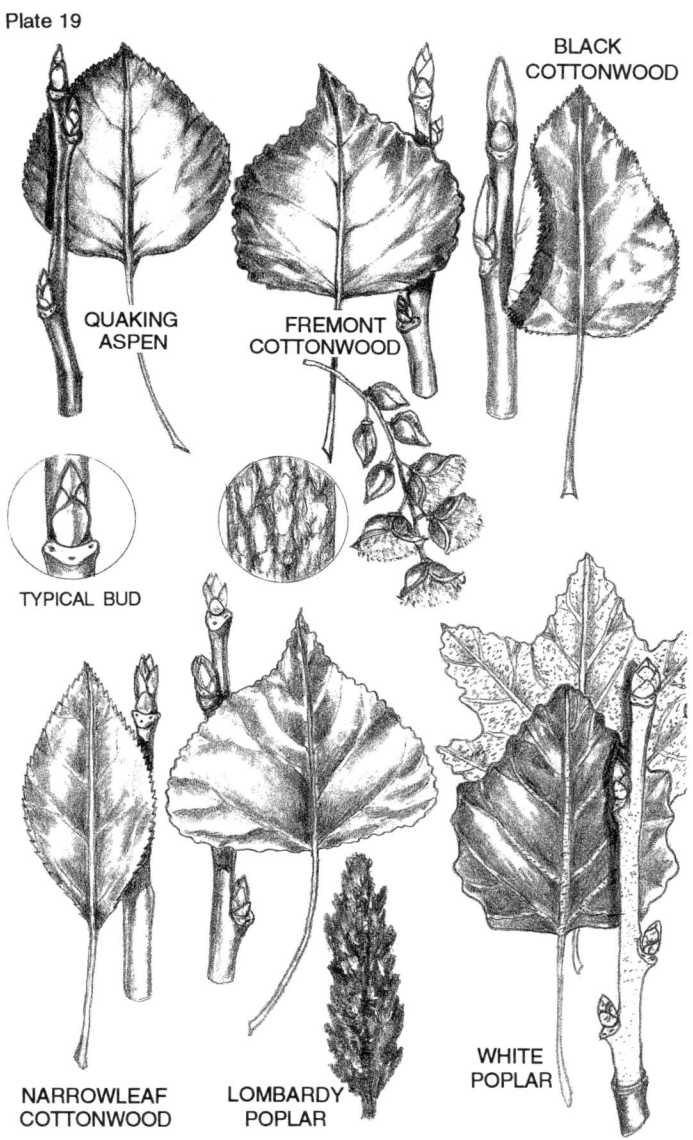

QUAKING
ASPEN

FREMONT
COTTONWOOD

BLACK
COTTONWOOD

TYPICAL BUD

NARROWLEAF
COTTONWOOD

LOMBARDY
POPLAR

WHITE
POPLAR

20. LEAVES MOSTLY DOUBLE-TOOTHED

Like willows and poplars (Plates 17-19), these trees bear flowers and fruits in slender catkins. Foliage is mostly *double-toothed* (but see White Alder). Mature female alder catkins are brown and woody, *like inch-long pine cones.* Alders are among the few non-legumes with root nodules that support nitrogen-fixing (soil-enriching) bacteria. Powdered alder bark is said to help control both diarrhea and external bleeding. Deer, beavers, and porcupines browse alder twigs or eat the inner bark; grouse feed on the buds. In this group, only Water Birch has spur branches.

WHITE ALDER *Alnus rhombifolia* Nutt.
Foliage variable, the leaf edges *single-toothed,* faintly double-toothed, or merely wavy-edged. Leaves egg-shaped, *hairless,* 2"- 5" long, with *9-12* pairs of major side veins. Twigs hairless; buds smooth, *blunt,* reddish, narrow-based (stalked), the 2-3 scales *not* overlapping. Trunk light gray with *broad* whitish markings to brown-scaly. Height to 80'. Moist sites to 8000'.

MOUNTAIN ALDER *Alnus incana* ssp.*tenuifolia* (Nutt.) Breit.
Like White Alder but leaves *decidedly* double-toothed and with *6-9* pairs of side veins. Some buds may lack a stalked base. Trunk bark with short *horizontal lines.* Height to 30'. Wet areas to 10,000' altitude. Also known as *A. tenuifolia.*

WATER BIRCH *Betula occidentalis* Hook.
Like Mountain Alder, this species has transverse *bark streaks.* The leaves, though, are only 1"- 3" long, often heart-shaped, and with *4-5* pairs of side veins. Twigs *rough-warty;* buds only 1/8" long, *pointed,* with 2-3 pairs of *overlapping* scales. Spur branches often *present.* Fruiting catkins dry, wide, but *not* woody or pineconelike. Bark aromatic. Height to 40'; elevations to 8000', mostly on eastern slopes. Those wild cherries (Plate 21) with spur branches have leaves single-toothed, twigs with a sour odor, and fruits fleshy.

CALIFORNIA HAZELNUT
Corylus cornuta var. *californica* (A. DC.) E. Murray
A *hairy-leaved* species with foliage *heart-shaped* or nearly circular. Twigs usually *hairy;* buds *blunt* with overlapping scales, the lowest ones *paired.* Fruits are tasty nuts in beaked husks 1"- 2" long. Trunk brown, unmarked. Height to 25', below 7000' elevation. Related to the European filbert.

Plate 20

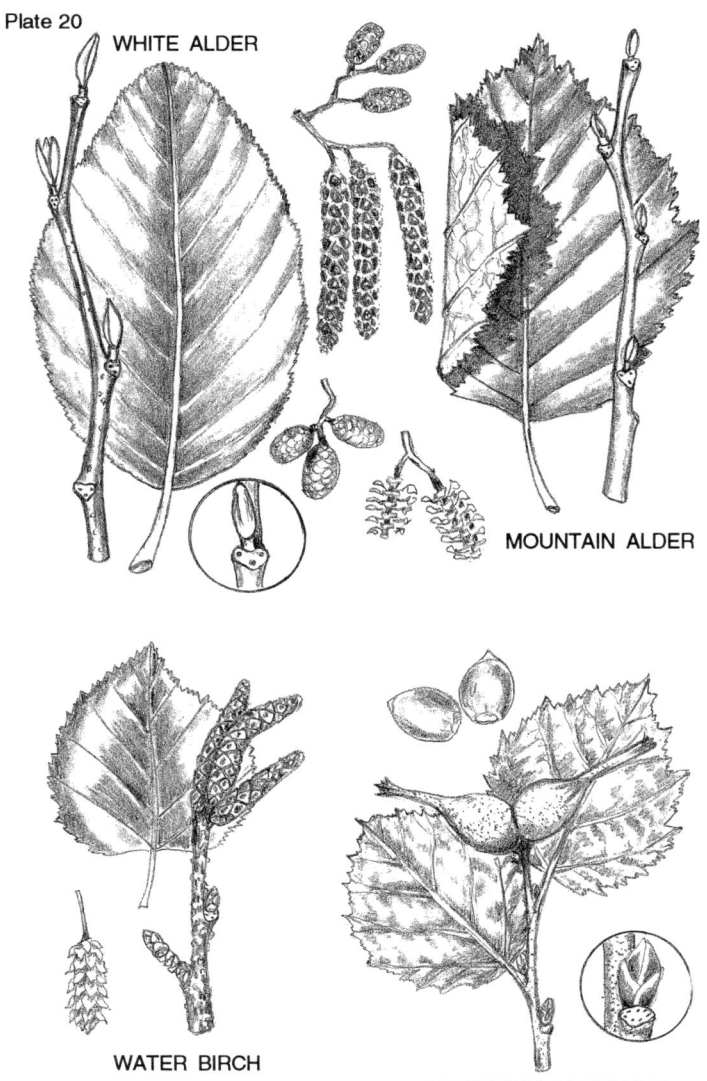

WHITE ALDER

MOUNTAIN ALDER

WATER BIRCH

CALIFORNIA HAZELNUT

21. LEAVES SINGLE-TOOTHED: PLUMS, CHERRIES

These trees have *fine-toothed* foliage and trunks mostly marked by *horizontal lines* (see also Mountain Alder and Water Birch, Plate 20). They have buds with several scales, bundle scars three, and leaf bases or leafstalks mostly with one or two tiny *glands.* Sierra Plum and Bitter Cherry usually have spur branches *present.* Sierra Plum has the end bud *false* (Fig. 2). Twigs mostly hairless and, especially in cherries, with a distinctive almond or *sour* odor when broken. Flowers small, white; fruits spherical, *fleshy, single-seeded.* Willows (Plate 18), poplars (Plate 19), White Alder (Plate 20), and species of Plate 22 also may have deciduous leaves single-toothed.

SIERRA PLUM *Prunus subcordata* Benth.
The only *deciduous* tree in the Sierras with strong, stubby twigs usually *spine-tipped.* Leaves 1"- 3" long, *sharp-toothed,* often heart-shaped or nearly *round.* Leafstalk glands sometimes lacking. Flowers in *umbrellalike* clusters, spring. Fruits yellowish to red, 1/4"- 1/2" wide, sour, summer. To 25' tall, on dry slopes below 6000'. Called Klamath Plum in Oregon. Hollyleaf Buckthorn (Plate 26) also has thorn-tipped twigs but is evergreen

BITTER CHERRY *Prunus emarginata* (Hook.) Walp.
Leaves 1"- 3" long, sometimes narrow, usually with tips *rounded,* and teeth rather *blunt.* Spring flowers in *short, rounded* groups; fruits 1/4"- 1/3" across, red to black, summer. To 20' tall, forming thickets at elevations below 9000'. Distributed mainly in the Pacific states and over much of British Columbia. Many animals eat the fruits despite their apparent bitter taste; mule deer browse the twigs.

CHOKE CHERRY *Prunus virginiana* var. *demissa* (Nutt.) Torr.
A transcontinental cherry with *2"- 4" elongated* flower/fruit clusters and *no* spur branches. Foliage 2"- 5" long, egg-shaped, *sharply* toothed, and tips *short-pointed.* Leafstalks often reddish. Flowers April-July; fruits purple to black, 1/4"- 1/3" in diameter, July-October. Height to 30', thickets and woods. Many birds and mammals consume the tart fruits; they are sometimes used for pies and jelly. Also named *P. demissa.*

Plate 21

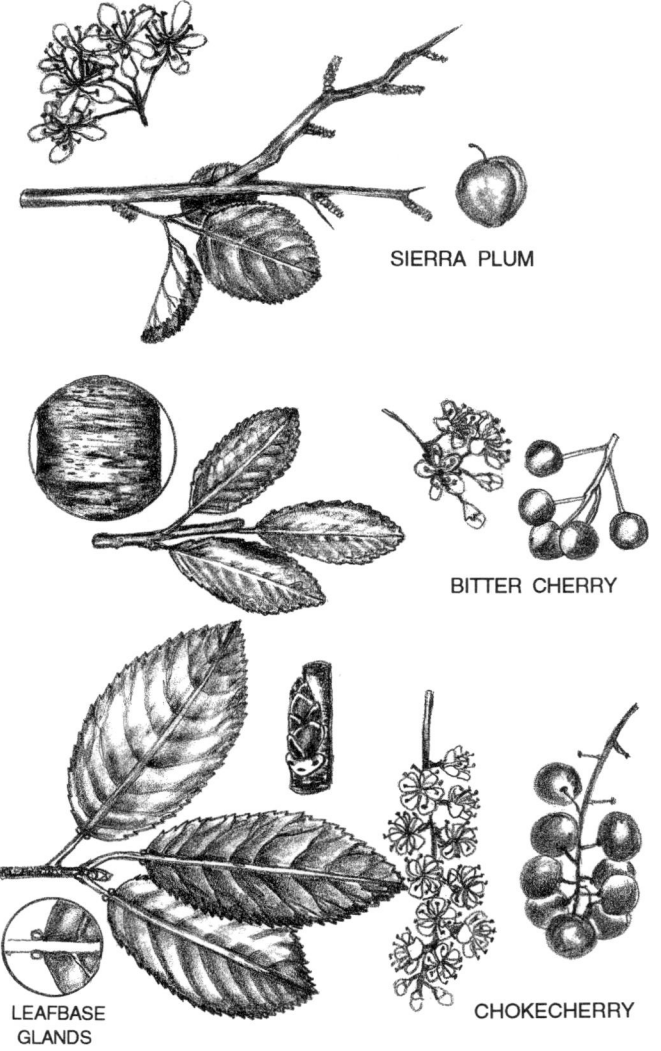

SIERRA PLUM

BITTER CHERRY

LEAFBASE
GLANDS

CHOKECHERRY

22. LEAVES MOSTLY SINGLE-TOOTHED: JUNEBERRIES AND BUCKTHORN

These species differ from those of Plate 21 in that horizontal lines on the trunk, glands on the leafstalk, and a distinctive odor from broken twigs are all *lacking.* They *do* have hairless twigs and three bundle scars per leaf scar but their fruits are *several-seeded* and their other characteristics are unlike those of cherries and plums. Note that Cascara Buckthorn may lack leaf teeth.

SERVICEBERRY (Saskatoon Juneberry)
Amelanchier alnifolia (Nutt.) Nutt.

A small tree or shrub with leaves *1"- 3"* long and *nearly circular.* There are 3 -20 pairs of *coarse teeth* mainly *toward the leaf tip* and *7-9* pairs of side veins mostly branched and *curved.* Leafstalks *1/2"- 1"* long. Buds purplish and *scaly;* spur branches usually *present.* Flowers *white,* clustered, attractive, with petals 3/8"- 5/8" long; April-June. Fruits juicy, tasty, *purplish,* and 1/4"- 1/2" wide; June-August. Height to 22'; open woods below 11,000'. Origin and meaning of Serviceberry name are uncertain (unless derived from Sorbusberry, see Plate 15). Western Juneberry and Alderleaf Juneberry are other names.

UTAH JUNEBERRY *Amelanchier utahensis* Koehne

A shrub or low tree similar to Serviceberry but leaves only *1/2"- 1 1/4"* long, including *1/4"- 1/2"* stalks. Flower petals and fruits also small, the former only 1/8"- 1/4" long and the latter just 1/8"- 1/4" in diameter. Slopes and canyons.

CASCARA BUCKTHORN *Rhamnus purshiana* DC

Well-known in the Pacific Northwest where the bark is harvested and marketed as a tonic and laxative. Leaves *3"- 6"* long, 1"- 2 1/2" wide, *fine-toothed* or sometimes without teeth, and with *10-15* pairs of *straight* and *parallel* lateral veins. Foliage and buds tend to be bunched near the twig tips (leaves sometimes nearly opposite) . Leaf tips *short-pointed* or blunt. Buds rusty-hairy, *without* scales; spur branches *lacking.* Flowers small, *greenish,* May-July; fruits fleshy, *black,* July-September. Trunk bark light gray, rather smooth. Height to 40'; moist woods below 5000' elevation. Fruits eaten by nearly all wildlife; mule deer consume the twigs.

Plate 22

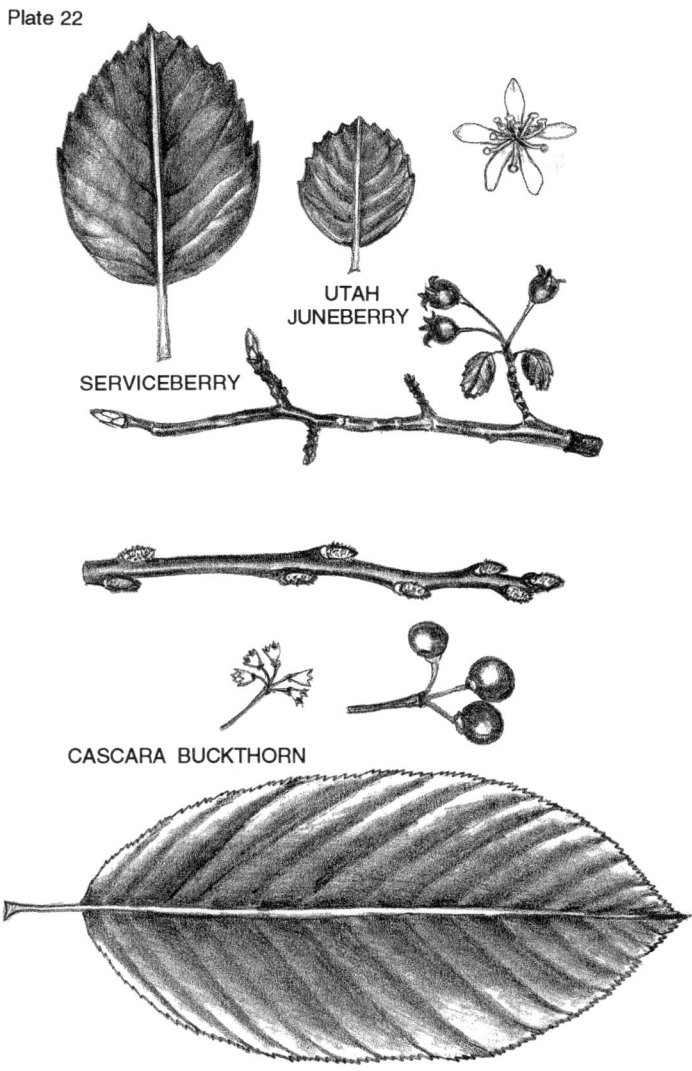

SERVICEBERRY

UTAH
JUNEBERRY

CASCARA BUCKTHORN

23. LEAVES FEATHER-LOBED AND BRISTLE-TIPPED: OAKS I

Regardless of foliage, oaks (Plates 20-23) can be identified by *end buds clustered* at the twig tips (but see also Cascara Buckthorn, Plate 22, and Golden Chinkapin, Plate 29). Oaks also have *more than three* bundle scars per leaf scar and, of course, bear *acorn* fruits. In late spring, male blossoms occur in slender, *drooping* catkins several inches long. Female flowers are small and unobtrusive. Acorns, green at first, become brown when mature. They are held in basal *cups* that, nevertheless, are commonly described as either bowl-shaped or saucerlike.

An oak species is most often classified as a member of either the red or white oak group. The lobe and leaf tips of red oaks have protruding hairlike *bristles* that are lacking in white oaks. Also, the acorns of red oaks take two years to mature while those of white oaks require only one. Thus, mature red oaks usually have developing acorns on the twigs *plus* older ones on the branchlets. White oak acorns, on the other hand, grow *only* on the twigs. In addition, the inner surface of the shells (not cups) of red oak acorns are *hairy* while those of white oaks are *not*. The meat of red oak acorns, too, usually contains much tannic acid and is bitter, while that of white oaks is light-colored and more edible. Canyon Live Oak (Plate 25), an exception to some of these guidelines, is called an intermediate oak.

Oaks are often valuable timber trees. Their acorns are essential in the diets of deer, squirrels, and many other wildlife species. Acorns also once served as important foods for Native Americans. Even the bitter acorns of red oaks were rendered edible by pounding the kernels and treating the flour with hot water. Reportedly, early settlers used dried acorn shells as a coffee substitute.

On this plate is the only deciduous member of the red oak group in the Sierra. Interior Live Oak (Pl. 25), also a red oak, is evergreen.

CALIFORNIA BLACK OAK *Quercus kelloggii* Newb.
The only wild oak in the Sierra with deeply lobed and *bristle- tipped* foliage. Leaves 4"- 7" long, with stalks *1"- 2"* long. Twigs occasionally hairy; buds about 1/4" in length, pointed, and hairless. Acorns 1"- 1 1/2" long with bowl-like cups. Trunk *dark*. Height to 75' (95'); diameter to 3' (4'). Mixed forests to 7000' elevation. Red oak species from the eastern United States, often planted for landscaping, have smaller acorns and either less-deeply lobed leaves or shorter leafstalks.

Plate 23

CALIFORNIA BLACK OAK

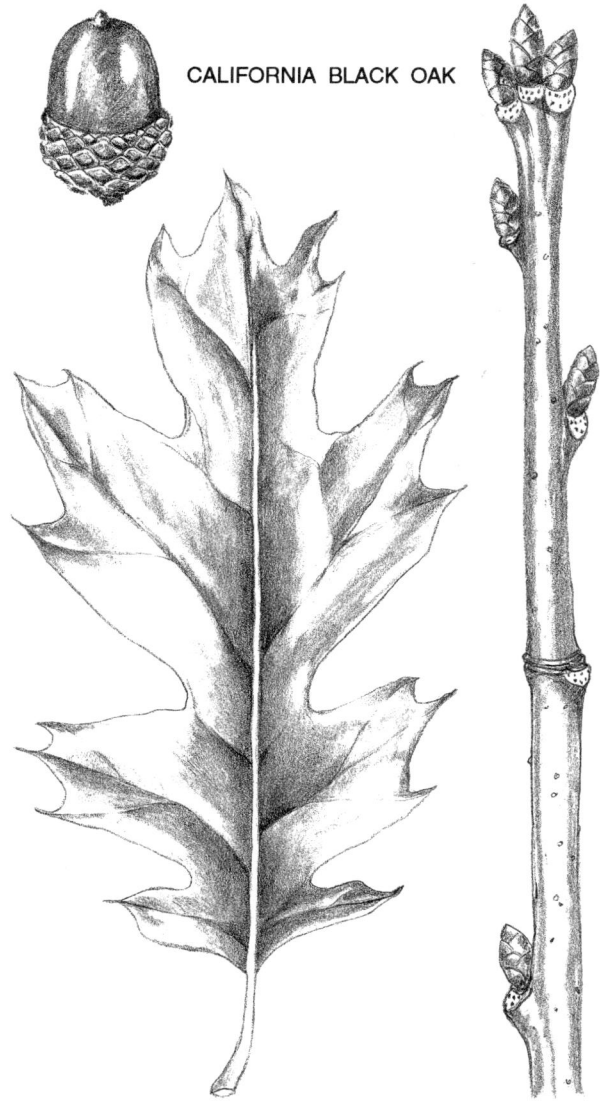

24. LEAVES MOSTLY FEATHER-LOBED WITHOUT BRISTLE-TIPS: OAKS II

These three deciduous oaks are mostly lobed-leaved members of the white oak group. They are the only white oaks in the Sierra (see Plate 23 for oak-group characteristics). Trunk bark *light gray.* In Spanish, roble (ROHB-leh) is the general name for a deciduous oak species; encino (en-SEEN-oh) is used for an evergreen oak.

OREGON OAK *Quercus garryana* Dougl. ex Hook
A species with *deeply-lobed* leaves 2"- 4" long, somewhat *leathery, glossy* above, usually *hairy* beneath. Leafstalks *1/2"- 1"* in length. Twigs frequently hairy; buds *1/4"- 1/2"* long, *pointed,* and *hairy.* Acorns 3/4"- 1 1/2" long with *shallow* cups. Although in some more northern and more coastal areas a tree to 90' tall with leaves 4"- 6" long, in the Sierra it is a shrub or small tree growing mainly at elevations under 5000'. Named after Nicholas Garry, an early Hudson's Bay Company officer and botanist. Often called Oregon White Oak.

VALLEY OAK *Quercus lobata* Née
Possibly the tallest western oak. Leaves 2"- 4" long, *deeply* lobed, *thin, dull,* and *hairless.* Leafstalks *1/4"- 1/2"* long. Twigs hairless and mostly *drooping;* buds about 1/4" in length, *pointed,* often hairy. Acorns 1 1/4"- 2" long with *deep* cups. Height to 100' (125'); diameter to 5' (13'). Rich soils, mostly under 2000' elevation. Also called Weeping Oak.

BLUE OAK *Quercus douglasii* Hook. & Arn.
The blue-green leaves vary in outline. They may be shallowly lobed, few-toothed, or smooth-edged. Foliage mostly *1"- 3"* long, pale bluish, *firm* but not leathery, sometimes hairy. May be evergreen on moist sites. Leafstalks only *1/8"- 3/8"* in length. Twigs *hairy;* buds *blunt, hairless,* 1/4" long. Acorns 3/4"- 1 1/2" in length; cups bowl-shaped. Tree 25'- 50' (90') tall and 1'- 2' (3') in diameter, on shallow rocky soils usually below 3500'. The scientific name memorializes David Douglas, the Scottish botanist of Douglas-fir (Plate 6) fame.

Plate 24

OREGON OAK

VALLEY OAK

BLUE OAK

25. EVERGREEN TREES WITH ACORNS AND CLUSTERED END BUDS: OAKS III

Called *live oaks* because of their evergreen foliage, these trees have leaves *thick*, rather *leathery*, often *hollylike*. Like all oaks, they produce acorns and have leaves and buds clustered at the twig tips. The first two species are true oaks. Their leaves are often *prickly-edged,* hollylike.The third, Tanoak, bears its flowers in a somewhat different pattern and is classified in a separate genus. Compare Blue Oak (Plate 24), whose firm foliage may be evergreen in some situations, and also Hollyleaf Buckthorn (Plate 26).

CANYON LIVE OAK *Quercus chrysolepis* Liebm.
    In canyons and on moist open slopes, this sometimes shrubby oak has small (1"- 2 1/2") leaves with edges either smooth or somewhat prickly. Foliage somewhat waxy and often whitened or *yellowish* beneath. Side veins mostly *parallel.* Acorn cups deep, thick-walled, and often *gold-hairy.* Called an intermediate oak because, like a red oak, the acorns require two years to mature and have hairy inner acorn shells (not cups). These fruits grow on wood, however, that does not normally produce new growth during the second year and thus *appear* to mature on twigs like white oaks. Trunk bark *grayish.* To 60' in height, mostly below 6500' elevation. The dense wood once was made into wedges and mauls (heavy hammers) to split logs. Maul Oak is an alternate name.

INTERIOR LIVE OAK *Quercus wizlizeni* A. DC.
    Mainly a tree of California's interior grasslands but also found on lower slopes of the Sierra Nevada. Leaves 1"- 2" long, prickly-edged or smooth, and *green* beneath, with veins mostly branching irregularly (parallel on some toothed leaves). Acorn cup *brownish* with thin walls. Trunk *dark.* Height to 65' at elevations under 7000'. A red oak.

TANOAK *Lithocarpus densiflorus* (Hook. & Arn.) Rehd.
    A large and mostly coastal tree, local and smaller in the Sierra. Leaves 2"- 5" long, whitish- to brownish-hairy beneath. Side veins *parallel* and leaf edges *sharply-toothed* but not prickly. Twigs and buds *yellow-hairy.* Male catkins *upright;* female blossoms small, at bases of male catkins. Acorns develop over a 2-year period in *saucerlike* cups decorated with *narrow, spreading* scales. Trunk *dark.* Height 50'- 100' (150'), diameter 1'- 3' (6'). Also called Tanbark-oak or merely Tanbark. Southern Asia is home to many *Lithocarpus* species.

Plate 25

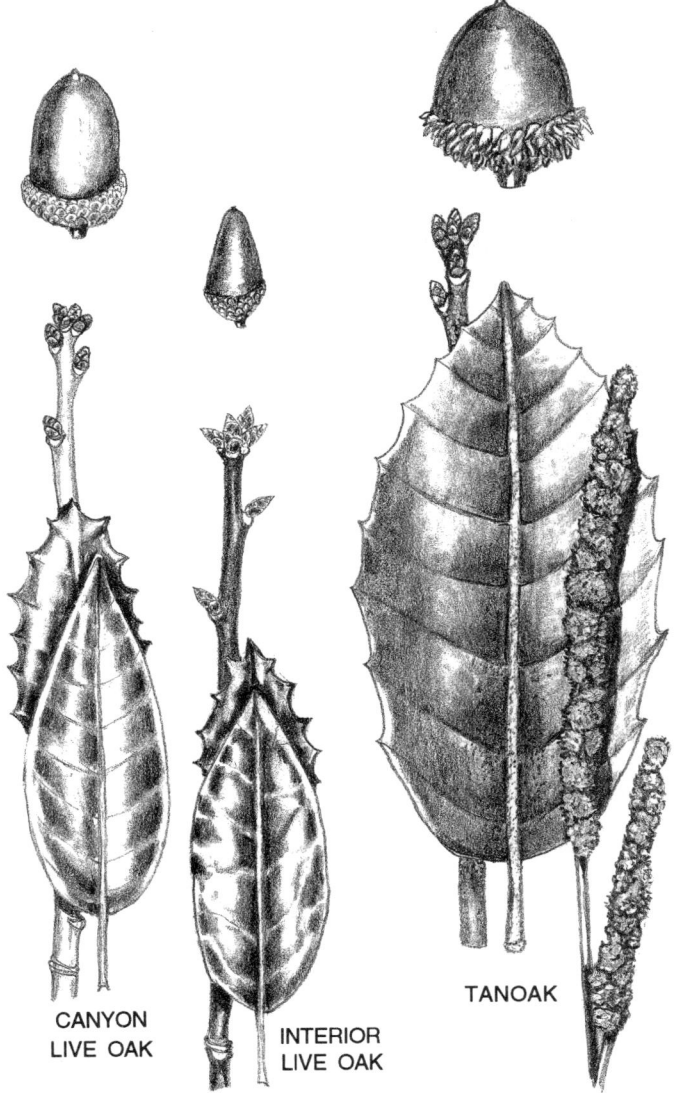

CANYON
LIVE OAK

INTERIOR
LIVE OAK

TANOAK

26. BROADLEAF EVERGREEN TREES WITH LEAVES TOOTHED

Except for the oaks of Plate 25, only these three Sierra trees have leathery evergreen foliage obviously toothed. Buds are *scaly*. All are easily recognized. In addition, California Fremontia (Plate 16) and the trees of Plate 27 *may* have some toothed leaves. Joshuatree Yucca (Plate 30) has leaf teeth so tiny that they must be tested with a fingernail or lens.

HOLLYLEAF BUCKTHORN *Rhamnus ilicifolia* Kellogg
The only broadleaf evergreen tree in the region with side twigs stiff and often *thorn-tipped*. Leaves 1/4"- 1/2" long, mostly *prickly-edged*, nearly *circular,* the lateral veins generally *parallel.* Spur branches may be *present.* Flowers tiny, yellow, April-May; fruits red, juicy, 2-seeded, June-July. Often shrubby but may grow to be 25' tall; elevations under 4000'. Part of *R. crocea* Nutt. complex. Sierra Plum (Plate 21), also thorny, is not evergreen. Canyon and Interior live oaks (Plate 25), also with evergreen prickly-edged foliage, have leaves larger and end buds clustered.

TOYON *Heteromeles arbutifolia* (Lindl.) Roem.
An ornamental tree or shrub. Leaves *2"- 5"* long, oval, *coarse-toothed,* long-stalked, hairless, and short-pointed. Spur branches *absent.* Flowers white, 1/4" across, in terminal clusters 4"- 6" long, June-July. Fruits fleshy, red, 1/4"- 3/8" in diameter, several-seeded, attractive, August-winter. Sometimes 35' tall; dry slopes to 4000' elevation. Known also as Christmasberry, Hollyberry, and California-holly. The fruits are consumed by bandtail pigeons, California quail, and other wildlife.

BIRCHLEAF CERCOCARPUS *Cercocarpus betuloides* Torr. & Gray
The long *feathery tails* on tiny fruits are most attractive. Leaves *3/4"- 1 1/2"* in length, *parallel-veined, wedge-based,* often velvet-hairy beneath, and toothed *above the middle.* Spur branches *frequent.* Flowers greenish, 1/4" wide in small groups, March-May; fruits single-seeded, narrow, dry, 1/2" long, with a silky-hairy plume 1 1/2- 4" in length. Height 15'- 25', on dry slopes to 10,000' elevation. Wood is often brownish and used in woodworking. It is heavy and will not float soon after being cut. Also called Mountain-mahogany, but not related to tropical mahoganies. Curlleaf Cercocarpus, Plate 28, is related. The name Cercocarpus is based on Greek for "tailed fruit". In the absence of fruits, compare California Buckthorn, Plate 27.

Plate 26

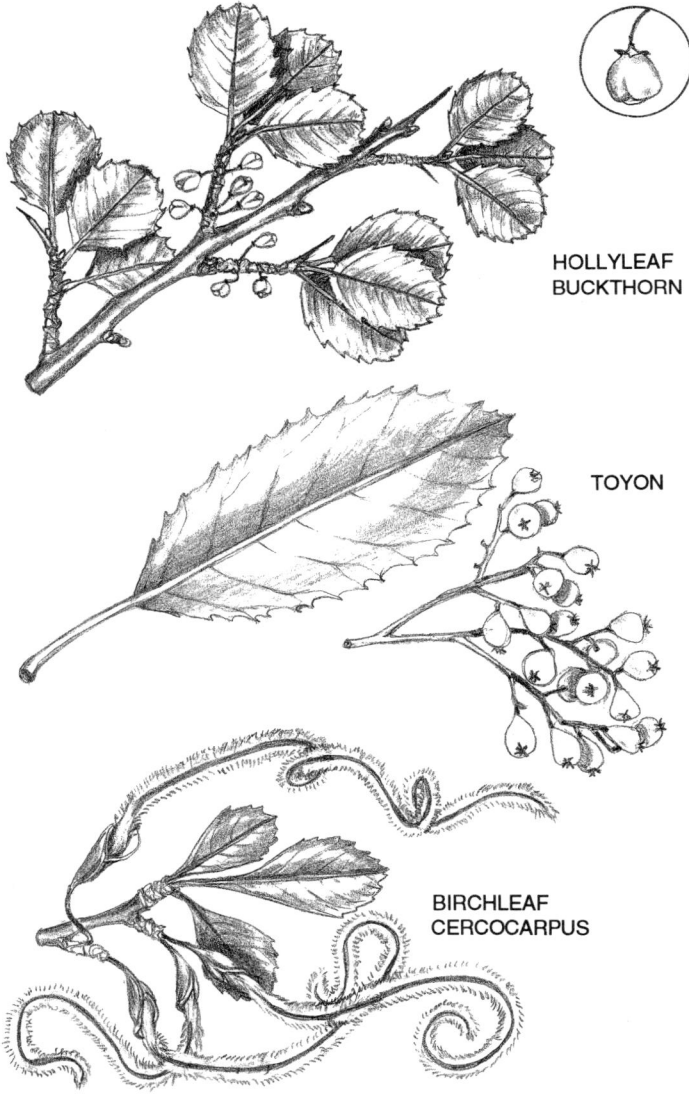

HOLLYLEAF
BUCKTHORN

TOYON

BIRCHLEAF
CERCOCARPUS

27. BROADLEAF EVERGREEN TREES WITH LEAVES SOMETIMES TOOTHED

Though most leaves are smooth-edged, the foliage of these two species, like that of California Fremontia (Plate 16), may sometimes show toothed borders. Leaves are *2"- 6"* long.

CALIFORNIA BUCKTHORN
Rhamnus californica Eschsch.

With variable foliage and *rarely* attaining tree size, this species has leaves 2"- 4" long and often *whitish* beneath. The foliage has *parallel* leaf veins, either U- or V-shaped bases, and is often fine-toothed (rarely with rather coarse teeth). Leaves occasionally opposite. Buds hairy and *without* scales. Spur branches *lacking*. Flowers greenish, March-April; fruits *black,* juicy, several-seeded, August-September. To 15' tall, on slopes below 4000' elevation. Frequently called California Coffeeberry. Unlike some related species (Plate 26), this buckthorn is not thorny.

PACIFIC MADRONE *Arbutus menziesii* Pursh

Well-known by its thin, *smooth, reddish-brown* bark on the upper trunk and large branches (see also Manzanitas, Plate 28), often peeling to show grayish-yellow underbark. Leaves 4"- 6" long, sometimes with fine teeth. Leaf bases U-, or occasionally, heart-shaped. Buds *scaly* and hairless. Flowers small, white, bell-shaped, in branched groups, March-May. Fruits red to orange, spherical, 1/4"- 1/2" wide, June-winter. Tree 25'- 80" (125') tall and 2'-3' (5') in diameter, at elevations beneath 5000'. Fruits are consumed by doves, bandtail pigeons, and ringtails. Deer browse the twigs. Bees collect nectar from the blossoms.

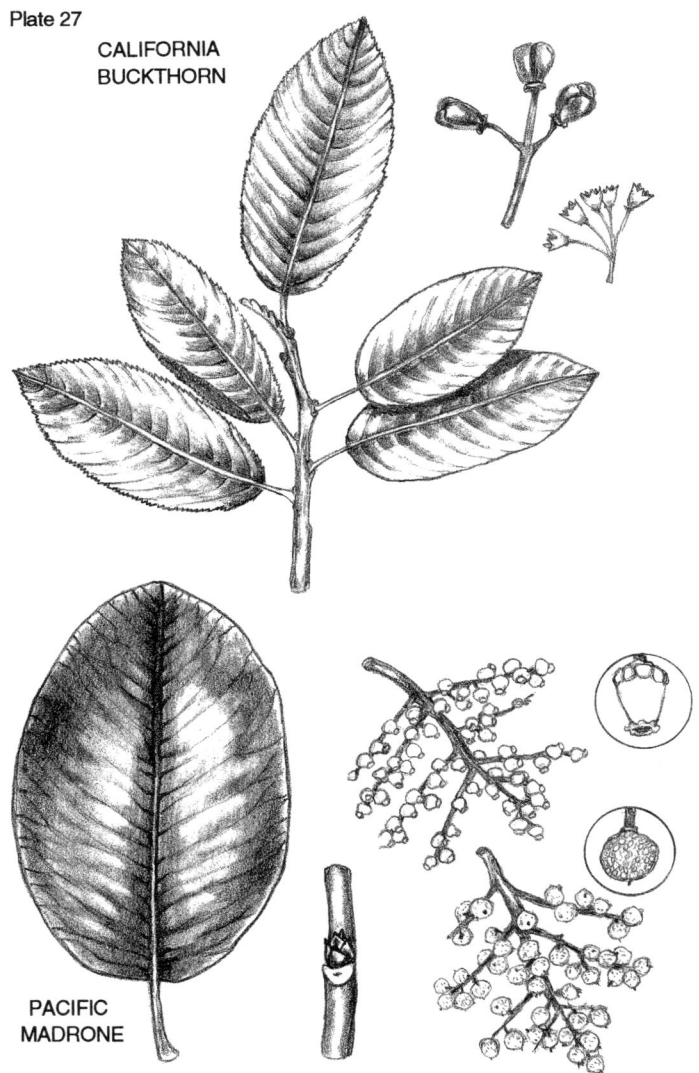

Plate 27

CALIFORNIA
BUCKTHORN

PACIFIC
MADRONE

28. BROADLEAF EVERGREEN TREES WITH SMALL LEAVES NOT TOOTHED

The foliage of these species is *thick, under two inches long,* and *without* teeth. See also California Fremontia, Plate 16.

CURLLEAF CERCOCARPUS *Cercocarpus ledifolius* Nutt.
A shrub or small tree of mountain slopes throughout the West. Leaves only *1/2"- 1 1/2"* long, short-stalked, sometimes hairy beneath, and with edges *curled under.* Spur branches *common.* Flowers without petals and inconspicuous. Fruits tiny but with interesting *feathery tails* 2"- 3" long. Mainly dry eastern slopes below 9000'. The heavy brown heartwood will not float but makes nice turned objects and leads to the alternate name of Mountain-mahogany. Mule deer browse the leaves and twigs. Birchleaf Cercocarpus (Plate 26), with leaves toothed, is related.

MANZANITAS *Arctostaphylos* species
A large genus mostly of crooked, shrubby plants. They have *smooth, bare, red-brown trunks* much the color and texture of Pacific Madrone (Plate 27). Leaves mostly hairless and only 1"- 2" long. Fruits spherical, fleshy or leathery, and mostly reddish. Manzanitas grow mainly on dry slopes below 5000' elevation.

Two species ranging mainly in the northern and central Sierra attain the 13' size of small trees. **Parry (Common) Manzanita** (*A. manzanita* C. Parry) has leaves *bright green,* twigs hairy or not, the mature fruits *5/16"- 1/2"* in diameter and not sticky. **Whiteleaf Manzanita** (*A. viscida* C. Parry) has foliage *whitened,* twigs sometimes hairy, fruits *1/4"- 3/8"* wide and either smooth or sticky.

Plate 28

CURLLEAF CERCOCARPUS

TYPICAL
MANZANITA

29. BROADLEAF EVERGREEN TREES WITH NARROW LEAVES NOT TOOTHED

Only two Sierra trees have foliage of this kind. Each has leaves *3"- 5"* long, hairless, and with bases mostly *V-shaped.*

CALIFORNIA BAY
Umbellularia californica (Hook. & Arn.) Nutt.
Leaves *either* short-pointed or with blunt tips. Foliage green and shiny above, *pale* beneath, and *aromatic* when crushed. Twigs also green and spicy-scented. Buds small, *without* scales. Flowers small, yellow, in umbrellalike groups, December-April. Fruits purplish, oval, 3/4"- 1" long, *smooth,* with a large seed, October-winter. Height 30'- 80', occurs to 6000' above sea level. Dried leaves are used to flavor food (but some people have unfavorable reactions!). Squirrels and jays consume the fruits. The lumber of large trees (now mostly harvested) makes fine furniture. Ornamental turned objects also are made from the wood. Also called Oregon-myrtle or California-laurel.

GOLDEN CHINKAPIN
Chrysolepis chrysophylla (Dougl. ex Hook.) Hjelmq.
Though shaped much like those of California Bay, the leaves of this species are *golden-yellow* beneath, *not* spicy, and with *sharp* tips. Twigs also yellow. Buds *scaly* and grouped at the twig ends. Flowers whitish, tiny. Fruits 4-parted, *prickly burs,* 1"- 1 1/2" long, that contain 1-3 angled nuts. Height 50'- 80' (130'); diameter 1'- 3' (4'), growing to 10,000' elevation. Mostly near the coast but also in the Lake Tahoe region and perhaps elsewhere in the Sierra. Formerly named *Castanopsis chrysophylla* (Dougl.) A.DC. Mule deer browse the foliage. Canyon Live Oak (Plate 25) also has end buds clustered and often yellowed foliage. Its leaves are smaller, frequently prickly-edged, however, and it has acorn fruits.

Plate 29

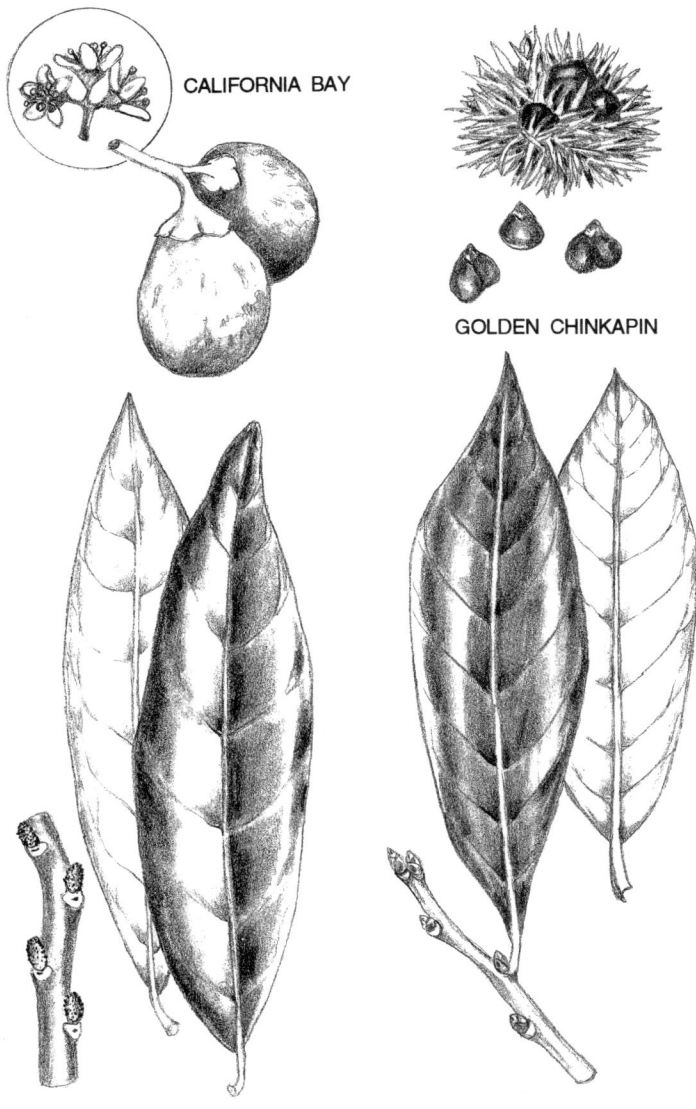

CALIFORNIA BAY

GOLDEN CHINKAPIN

30. EVERGREEN TREES WITH STIFF PARALLEL-VEINED LEAVES: YUCCAS

With dense clusters of thick, fibrous, *bayonet-shaped,* and *spine-tipped* leaves, yuccas are unique. Most species are shrubby; a few grow to be trees. Dead leaves usually cover the trunks. Springtime blossoms are large, white, and occur in *showy* upright clusters 1'- 2' long. Fruits are leathery, cylindrical, and 2"- 4" long. In California, yuccas occur at low elevations in arid districts. Two tree species are found where the southern Sierra borders the Mohave Desert.

Native Americans ate the flowers, buds, and young flower stalks. They also consumed the raw or roasted fruits and made them into a flour that was baked into cakes for storage. Leaf fibers were woven into baskets, ropes, mats, sandals, and coarse blankets. Attractive baskets are still made from green, yellow, and white fibers taken from various parts of the leaves.

In a remarkable example of mutually beneficial relationships in nature, the late J. D. Laudermilk of Pomona College, California, observed that the female yucca moth feeds on the nectar of yucca blossoms and, at the same time, collects pollen. Deliberately, she places an egg in each of several ovules in a flower's ovary. In moving about, she applies pollen to the flower's stigma, thus insuring fertilization and seed growth. The growing moth larvae feed on some of the developing seeds and, upon reaching maturity, repeat the pollenization cycle that enables both species to survive.

JOSHUATREE YUCCA *Yucca brevifolia* Engelm.
> A *branched* and very treelike yucca. It is the yucca with the *shortest* leaves and the only one with foliage that, upon close examination, shows *finely-toothed* leaf borders (use a lens or scratch the leaf edge). Leaves only *6"- 13"* long and *1/4"-1/2"* wide. Single blossoms *2"- 3"* long, in clusters 6"- 15" in length. Parts of the trunk sometimes bare. Height to 50', dry soils below 4000' elevation. Woodpeckers may excavate nest holes in the trunk. Many wild animals consume the fruits. The rootlets were once used to make a red dye.

MOHAVE YUCCA *Yucca schidigera* K. E. Ortgies
> A smaller yucca mostly *not extensively* branched. Leaves *16"- 32"* long and *1"- 2"* wide, with edges showing obvious *loose fibers.* Flowers *1"- 2"* long, in clusters 12"- 24" in length. Grows to be 20' tall at elevations of 1000'-5000'.

Plate 30

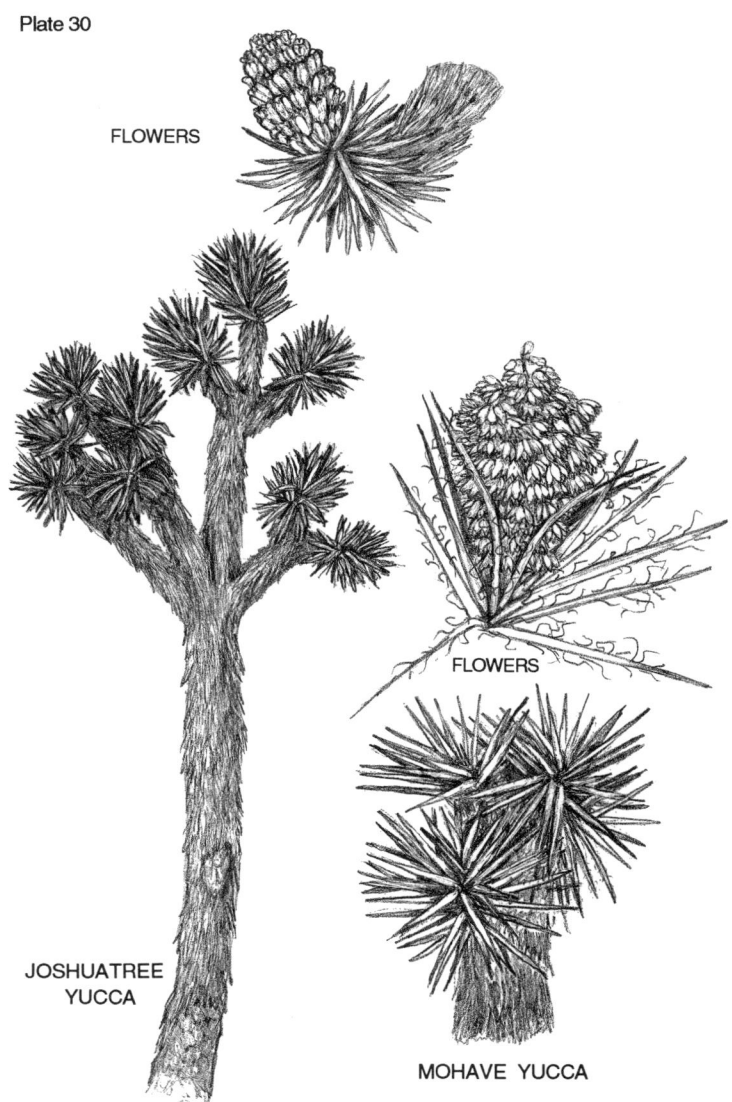

FLOWERS

FLOWERS

JOSHUATREE
YUCCA

MOHAVE YUCCA

KEY TO TREES IN LEAFLESS CONDITION

Each key item is a couplet. Compare the unknown specimen with the first two choices. Select the alternative that agrees with the specimen and proceed to the couplet number indicated. Repeat until a final determination is reached. Use a lens when necessary.

1. Leaf scars opposite or whorled (Sections II and III of text). **2**
1. Leaf scars alternate (Sections IV and V of text). **10**
    2. Leaf scars meeting in raised points.   **Ashleaf Maple Pl 12**
    2. Leaf scars not meeting in raised points. **3**
3. Buds without scales, hairy; buds and leaf scars opposite mostly
        near twig tips.   **Cascara Buckthorn Pl.22**
3. Buds scaly. **4**
    4. Bud scales 2, meeting.   **Maples Pl.13, Dogwood etc.Pl.14**
    4. Bud scales several, overlapping. **5**
5. Central end bud missing, a single pair of buds usually present
        at twig tips; bundle scars 3 or more. **6**
5. Central end bud present, often flanked by side buds. **7**
    6. Twigs stout, pith wide.   **Elderberries Pl.11**
    6. Twigs slender, pith narrow.   **Sierra Bladdernut Pl. 12**
7. Leaf scars often whorled, bundle scar one,
        fruits brown inch-wide balls.   **Buttonbush Pl. 14**
7. Leaf scars paired, bundle scars more than one. **8**
    8. Bundle scars 3, buds scaly or white-hairy,
        fruits in winged pairs.   **Maples Pl. 13**
    8. Bundle scars many, often in 3 groups. **9**
9. Buds with obvious scales, fruits shiny brown nuts in husks.
        California Buckeye Pl. 9
9. Buds smooth, granular; fruits single-winged.   **Ashes Pl. 10**
    10. Trees with one of the following (a-i) unique characteristics:
      a. Buds clustered at the twig tips.   **Oaks Pls. 23-24**
      b. Buds without scales.   **Cascara Buckthorn Pl. 22**
      c. Buds with a single, smooth, caplike scale.
          California Sycamore Pl. l6; Willows Pls.17-18
      d. Leaf scar O-shaped, surrounding bud.
          California Sycamore Pl. 16
      e. Leaf scar U-shaped, nearly surrounding bud.
          California Hoptree Pl. l2
      f. Catkins like inch-long pine cones, usually present; buds
        blunt with 2-3 scales not overlapping.   **Alders Pl. 20**
      g. Pith chambered.   **Hinds Walnut Pl.15**
      h. Leaf scars 1/4"- 3/4" deep, triangular; twigs thick,
        pith solid.   **Tree-of-Heaven Pl. 15**
      i. Side twigs spiny or stubby.   **Sierra Plum Pl. 21**
    10. Trees lacking any of the distinctive (a-i) characteristics. **11**

11. Buds with lowermost scale centered directly above the leaf scar; bark often smooth and greenish on young trunk and branches; spur branches occasional. **Poplars Pl. 19**
11. Bud scales and trunk bark otherwise. **12**
    12. Spur branches absent. **13**
    12. Spur branches usually present (see also Poplars Pl.19). **14**
13. Buds few-scaled, the lowest scales larger and paired; twigs usually hairy; fruits nuts. **California Hazelnut Pl 20**
13. Buds many-scaled, twigs hairless, fruits pods. **California Redbud Pl. 16**
    14 . Trunk marked with short horizontal lines, bundle scars 3, fruits dry or fleshy. **15**
    14. Trunk bark without horizontal lines, bundle scars 3 or 5, fruits fleshy. **16**
15. Buds with 2-3 scales, broken twigs without an almond odor, fruits catkins. **Water Birch Pl. 20**
15. Buds with 4-6 scales, broken twigs often with an almond odor, fruits juicy. **Cherries Pl. 21**
    16. Bundle scars 3; buds long-pointed, purplish, scales often twisted with black notched tips, second bud scale usually under half length of bud; fruits purple. **Juneberries Pl. 22**
    16. Bundle scars 5, buds stout, reddish; fruits orange or red. **Mountain-ashes Pl. 15**

REFERENCES

Gerstenberg, R.H. 1983. *Common Trees and Shrubs of Southern Sierra Nevada.* Reedley, Calif., Kings River College.

Hickman, James C. (edit.) 1993. *The Jepson Manual: Higher Plants of California.* Berkeley, Univ. Calif. Press.

Jepson, Willis Linn 1923. *The Trees of California,* 2nd ed. Berkeley, (Univ. Calif.) Associated Students Store.

Little, Elbert L., Jr. 1979. *Checklist of United States Trees (Native and Naturalized).* Washington: Agri. Handbook 541, Forest Service, U.S. Dept. Agri.

McMinn, Howard E. and Evelyn Maino. 1980. *An Illustrated Manual of Pacific Coast Trees.* Berkeley, Univ. Calif. Press.

Morin, Nancy R. (edit.). 1993, 1997. *Flora of North America,* vols. 2 and 3. Oxford Univ. Press, New York.

Petrides, George A. and Olivia Petrides 1992, 1998. *A Field Guide to Western Trees.* Houghton Mifflin Co. Boston, Massachusetts.

Muir, John. 1913. *The Mountains of California.* New York: Century Company.

Munz, Philip A. and David D. Keck. 1968. *A California Flora.* Berkeley, Univ. Calif. Press.

Peterson, P. Victor and P. Victor Peterson, Jr. 1975. *Native Trees of the Sierra Nevada.* Berkeley, Univ. Calif. Press.

Petrides, George A. and Olivia Petrides. 1992. *A Field Guide to Western Trees.* Houghton Mifflin Co., Boston, Mass. 02108

Weeden, N. 1981. *A Sierra Nevada Flora.* Berkeley, Wilderness Press.

INDEX TO PLATES

CALIFORNIA
and the Sierra Nevada

Mt. Shasta
7
9
10
Eureka
1
11
11
12
12
SIERRA NEVADA
13
13
Lake Tahoe
14
14
15
16
20
15
2
White Mountains
3a
San Francisco
17
SIERRA
18
3
4
8
18
NEVADA
19
6
Los Angeles
5
Salton Sea
San Diego

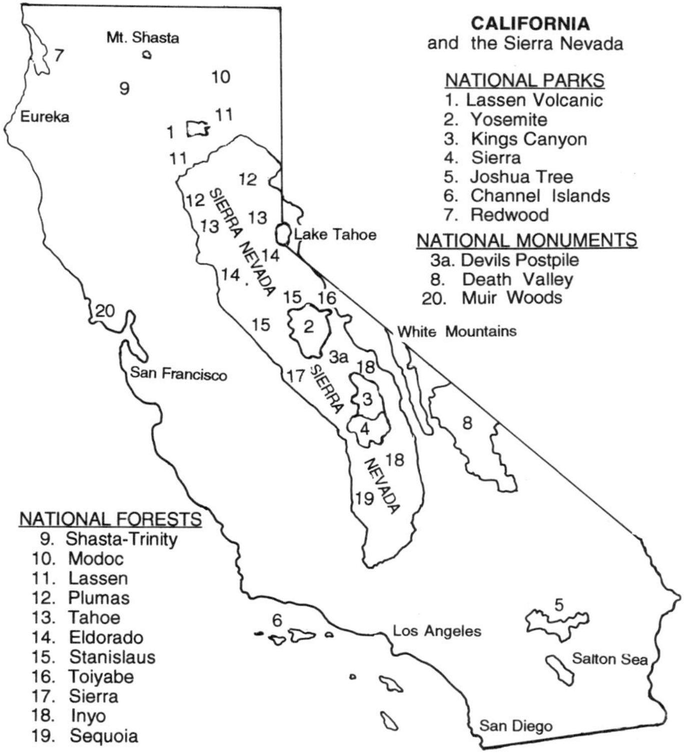

NATIONAL PARKS
1. Lassen Volcanic
2. Yosemite
3. Kings Canyon
4. Sierra
5. Joshua Tree
6. Channel Islands
7. Redwood

NATIONAL MONUMENTS
3a. Devils Postpile
8. Death Valley
20. Muir Woods

NATIONAL FORESTS
9. Shasta-Trinity
10. Modoc
11. Lassen
12. Plumas
13. Tahoe
14. Eldorado
15. Stanislaus
16. Toiyabe
17. Sierra
18. Inyo
19. Sequoia

INCHES
0
1
2
3
4
0
1
2
3
4
5
6
7
8
9
10
CENTIMETERS

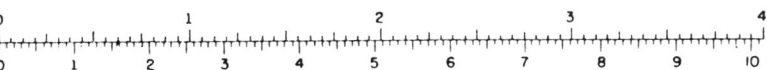